"An easy, quick read that gets right to the point. It's loaded with easy to implement organizing tips that will make you wonder why you waited so long to get organized!"
- Barry Izsak, CPO®, CRTS, Past President National Association of Professional Organizers, Author of *Organize Your Garage In No Time* and Owner of ArrangingItAll.com

" I am a big fan of making things simple! Becky's expert advice is fun to read and will simplify your life. "
- Sherie Dodsworth, CEO of Securita, creator of the Vital Records PortaVault®

"Change your life with Becky Esker! Take two minutes a day to implement what Becky teaches and create your own miracles."
- Elizabeth Hagen, Speaker, Coach and Author of *Organize With Confidence*; www.ElizabethHagen.com

"Becky Esker has spelled out how to organize your life from January through December and from A to Z! Practical, realistic, and achievable solutions to life's most nagging organizing issues are wrapped up on this amazing book - a must read for everyone!"
- Patty Kreamer, CPO®, Author of *But I Might Need It Someday*, President of Kreamer Connect, Inc and Organized A to Z

2 Minute Organizing Miracles
Simple Secrets to Leading an Organized Life

Becky Esker, CPO®

2 Minute Organizing Miracles: Simple Secrets to Leading an Organized Life

This publication is designed to provide accurate and authoritative information in regard to the subject matter covered. It is sold with the understanding the publisher and copyright owner are not engaged in rendering legal, accounting or other professional service. If legal advice or other expert assistance is required, the services of a competent professional person who specializes in that particular field should be sought.

While due care has been taken in the compilation of this publication, we are not responsible for errors or omissions. This reference is intended to assist in providing information to the public, and the information is delivered as accurately as possible.

Please direct any comments, questions, or suggestions regarding this publication to:
Get Organized! L.L.C.
P.O. Box 10827
Cedar Rapids, Iowa 52410
319-395-7477
info@getorganizedcr.com

To my father, Max S. Wolfe, who died way too young, but made an extraordinary impact on so many people.

I miss you Daddy!

Contents

●●●

1   Why Get Organized?   p. 19

2   What Do I Need To Be Organized For The Long Haul?   p. 22

3   The #1 Organizing Myth   p. 26

4   The Top Organizing Secret   p. 29

5   The Daily Grind: Mail & Paperwork   p. 34

6   Help, Sticky Notes Everywhere!   p. 37

7   SOS! It's Tax Time   p. 40

8   Magazine Madness   p. 44

9   Laundry: The Spin Cycle!   p. 47

10   Organizing: All Work, No Play?   p. 50

11   Container Invasion   p. 53

12   Official Diagnosis: Surface Clutter   p. 57

13 Turn Over a New Spring Leaf   p. 61

14 What is it about Shopping?   p. 64

15 Help Me! I C-A-N-'T Let Go   p. 67

   S-WEE-P™   p. 68

   Time & Energy Bandits   p. 70

   Weeding Out   p. 73

   Essential Questions:
   Ask Yourself   p. 75

   6 Steps to Reduce Your Stuff   p. 76

   A Holiday for Letting Go   p. 78

16 Can I Make $$$ from My Stuff?   p. 81

   Garage Sale, Today!   p. 83

   Write It Off   p. 85

   To Consign, or Not to Consign?   p. 87

17 Garage Disasters!   p. 90

18 It's Travel Time – Bon Voyage!   p. 93

   Toll Free Numbers   p. 99

	Airlines	p. 99
	Automobile Rentals	p. 100
	Hotels & Motels	p. 100
	International Working Cell Phones	p. 102
19	Organizing Your Kids	p. 103
20	Back to School Rules	p. 105
21	Tangled in the Tinsel	p. 109
	Six Holiday Organizing Ideas	p. 109
	How to FINALLY Get Organized for the New Year	p. 112
22	Don't Shop 'Till You Drop!	p. 115
23	You Can't Take It with You	p. 118
24	Think: Multi-Use	p 121
25	Holy Cow: What God Says About Clutter!	p. 124
26	Organize Your Financial Health	p. 127
27	Get a Grip on Spending	p. 130
28	Think Outside the Box	p. 133

29	Set S.M.A.R.T. Organizing Goals	p. 136
30	Get Yourself a "Nag Buddy"	p. 139
31	To-Do List Master	p. 142
32	Don't let the Demands of Your Job Manage You	p. 147
33	Yet Another Business Meeting	p. 152
34	The True Cost of Paper	p. 156
35	Make the Most of Limited Workspace	p. 159
36	Please, Stop the Interruptions	p. 162
37	Five Strategies to Improve Productivity	p. 165
38	De-Stress - For the HEALTH of It	p. 169
39	One Week to a Clean Desk	p. 173
40	Attack Your Reading Pile	p. 176
41	Stop the Screen and Let Me Off	p. 180
42	Hoarding vs. Clutter	p. 184
43	Should I Hire an Organizer?	p. 187

Appendix 1 References   p. 190

Appendix 2 Resources   p. 192

Appendix 3 Summary of Organizing Tips   p. 193

Appendix 4 Products   p. 206

About the Author   p. 207

Acknowledgements

●●●

I would like to thank my extraordinary team who helped bring this book to fruition: Pat Roland and Sally Ficken who met with me week after week for months on end, Kristy Shreeves for her wonderful editorial suggestions, Julie Perrine for holding me accountable and Amber O'Connor for taking on the final editing. Without these folks this book would not have made it to final copy.

A special thanks also goes to those who contributed to the content: Anita Van Dyke and Liz Van Antwerp for chapters 14 and 33 and the Just For Organizers readers who contributed many of the Quick Tips.

I would be horribly remiss if I overlooked my professional organizing industry colleagues: Barry Izsak, Elizabeth Hagen, Patty Kreamer, Brenda Spandrio, Sherie Dodsworth and Harold Taylor for taking time to preview my work and share their comments.

Lastly, I give my heartfelt thanks to my husband Don, daughter Madison and son Blake for allowing me to devote hours upon hours to this book and my career.

Foreword

    Like most people, I grew up with a much skewed idea of what it meant to be organized. My father was compulsively on top of things – but his desk was a mess. My mother cleaned obsessively and abhorred clutter – but closets and drawers were crammed full of stuff. My younger brother was ADHD and I was "normal" – whatever that is!! I grew to believe that organized meant clutter-less with everything perfectly filed or lined up on a labeled shelf. After several years of watching Becky Esker work, I have learned a few things. First, organized simply means you can put your hands on what you want or need immediately. Organized means everything has a home – a place for everything. And finally, regardless of your upbringing, your education or your temperament, you can always benefit from learning new and better ways to get organized!

    Becky and I have collaborated on a number of projects. We've worked together with a wide variety of people including start up business owners, hyperactive executives, compulsive hoarders, and women entrepreneurs with busy families. I came to appreciate her "no nonsense" approach when dealing with the whirl of emotions that come with chronic disorganization. I don't know anyone who has researched this subject more or worked harder in this field. Becky has been sharing tips on getting organized through speaking and writing for years. This book is a wonderful resource on how to get started and how to maintain an organized life.

"Laura" was a highly intelligent woman working in healthcare. She contacted Becky's business Get Organized because her marriage was on the rocks due to her hoarding. Becky and her staff had worked for days helping this woman clear a path through her house by the time they called me in to help with the emotional turmoil she was experiencing. As a clinical psychologist and coach, I had seen hoarding before, but this case was particularly challenging. "Laura" had to look at every item and weigh which was best before selecting what to keep and what to give or throw away. Parting with even a sticky rubber spatula evoked tears. After weeks of working with "Laura", we discovered she had continued shopping compulsively, hiding stuff in places like the trunk of her car. There are thousands of men and women like "Laura" out there who need the support of professionals to change their lives. Compulsive hoarding is an extreme. Most of us simply struggle with too much stuff, too much clutter, and too little structure and discipline in our busy lives. All this busy-ness and lack of organizational skill makes us inefficient and the stress grows. I personally believe we seriously underestimate what disorganization costs us in time, money, and peace of mind. You may not have a problem as extreme as hoarding or compulsive shopping or ADHD. You may simply be wasting hours on end dealing with e-mail, taking days and days to file your taxes, or are unable to find your passport when the opportunity to get away comes. 2 Minute Organizing Miracles will help you find the solutions you need.

Every personality type has its organizational Achilles heel. Analytical-types tend to be the best at keeping their world in order, but create overly complicated systems that no one can maintain. Drivers and Expressives are too busy running ahead and inspiring others to pay attention to the details of organizing. Amiable-types resist rocking the boat, and try to keep everyone happy, and so they quietly go mad trying to keep order. Knowing your personal strengths and weaknesses includes knowing where you need help and getting it. Applying the principles of this book will put you on track for creating the life you've always wanted. I challenge you to keep reading and begin applying what you learn so you can Get Organized!

Dr. Lisa Van Allen
The Biz Doctor
www.VanAllenCoaching.com

Preface
●●●

This book offers suggestions and ideas for getting, and staying organized. However, just as individuals are unique, so are the strategies that work for each person. Much of this book is geared toward "traditional" organizing methods. Those with right dominant brains, or ADHD, may not necessarily find all strategies to be best suited for them and their personal way of thinking. However, all readers will discover a basic underlying of structured ideas and systems. It is this structure that provides exactly what right-brainers, and those with ADHD, need to be successful at organization!

Beginning with Chapter 31, you will find strategies and ideas that can be applied primarily to an office environment. While specific to the working world, many of these tips can be easily and successfully transferred and utilized in a home environment, too.

Life is complex and confusing in so many ways. Many of us no longer have large chunks of time available for reading. Therefore, I have intentionally written small and to-the-point chapters. My goal, with each of you in mind, is to offer something that is a quick and easy read. So, feel free to pick up and read just a chapter at a time. Each chapter or subchapter should take you no more than about two minutes to read, and bit by bit you will be on your way!

The book is also intended to be used as a personal reference guide. For example, you might want to re-read the "Tangled in Tinsel" chapter every fall as you prepare for the upcoming holiday season. Or, should you decide to hold a garage sale, you would surely want to reference the "Can I Make Money from My Stuff" chapter and pay particular attention to the garage sale checklist! Whatever your need, my hope is that you will find a chapter to steer you in the right direction and lead you one step closer to your goal.

Please enjoy the book and take 2 Minutes to Get Organized!

Becky Esker

Chapter 1

WHY GET ORGANIZED?

"The single best reason to get organized is for the inner peace it will bring."

-Pam Young and Peggy Jones (The Slob Sisters)

What is the benefit of organizing anyway? Many of my organizing seminars start out with this very question. Whenever I pose this question to an audience, many hands shoot up. I often hear responses such as: you can find things, you feel better about yourself, you are less frustrated, you lower your blood pressure, you have more time, you are less overwhelmed, and the list goes on and on.

There are truly three major benefits of organizing that I consistently reference. Let's take a look at them:

1) Saves Time and Money. According to the Wall Street Journal, one hour is wasted everyday simply because of disorganization. By converting this to a 24-hour day, one hour wasted each day equates to 15 full days a year. That's like a full two-week vacation each year dedicated to disorganization! It is simply astounding.

From a business perspective, it is just as daunting. Applying one hour per week to a 40-hour work week equates to six weeks per work year wasted on disorganization. Wow! Think about how much this truly costs an employer. Let's assume a salary of $50,000 per year. Six weeks of pay at this salary is equal to $6,000. That is $6,000 in cold hard cash lost to disorganization for just one employee! This is money the employer can never get back.

Have I got your attention, yet? Here is another way of looking at the cost of disorganization. What happens if you know you have something in your house, yet you can't find it? Well, the majority of people will simply go buy another one. Bingo! Yet, another cost to both time and money.

2) Less Stress. I know you can relate to the awful feeling you have when you can't find something. Or, how about the frustration of running around like a chicken with its head cut

off? Simply put, the more organized you are - the less stress you have. Being organized eliminates middle of the night panic attacks when you suddenly realize "OH MY GOSH, I forgot to _____."

3) Success. This is the third, and final, benefit I like to reference. If you are organized, you are going to be successful in whatever task or project you are tackling. Whether it is something as simple as getting dinner on the table by 6:00 p.m., or completing a major project at work, success is within your reach.

Always keep the benefits in mind and you will find reaching your goals will be as simple as one, two, and three.

> *QUICK TIP: Organizing gives you more time to do what you love. Chances are good the first thing you want to do at the end of the day or on the weekend does not involve managing piles or dealing with clutter. So this is one of the most powerful motivations for getting (and staying) organized: when you no longer have to devote time, thought, and energy to corralling the excess stuff around you, you can devote that time, thought, and energy to the people, activities, and events that you love.*
>
> **Emily Wilska, The Organized Life**
> **San Francisco, California**

Chapter 2

WHAT DO I NEED TO BE ORGANIZED FOR THE LONG HAUL?

"People often say that motivation doesn't last. Well, neither does bathing -- that's why we recommend it daily."

-Zig Ziglar

So, you want to get organized…but where do you start? Take it one step further and you'll soon be wondering how you actually stay organized once you get there? First of all, organization is not a destination. Let me repeat that, organization is not a destination.   Rather, organization is an ongoing process. Organization requires constant maintenance and tweaking on your part.

There are three integral requirements for getting and staying organized.

First is a commitment. You must personally commit to get organized and to the follow through of staying organized. Failing to make a personal commitment means failure to reach your goal of an organized project. Let's face it, nothing organizes itself! Organization requires discipline from within, and positive self-talk is absolutely critical to this first step of the process.

Second is an investment. You must be willing to invest some amount of money. For what, you ask? For supplies, specific products, and in some instances to invest in assistance. Organizing is a learned skill. Some people have more of a natural knack than others. Others simply need to be taught. If you simply need to be taught, investing in the services of a professional organizer, who can teach and transfer those skills, can be a very wise investment. Additionally, if you have the skills, but simply have too much backlog to tackle on your own, a professional organizer can be the best solution to getting back on track.

Many people think, "If I buy this or that particular organizing supply, I will get organized." Unfortunately, this rarely works and you simply end up with a bunch of organizing books and products adding to your already-cluttered space. It is important to remember that organizing supplies are simply tools. If you don't know how to utilize and implement the tools, then you will find yourself utterly discouraged among a mass of clutter. A professional organizer can really help determine what products are needed and then teach you how to use them correctly.

Third, is devoting time. This component really pulls everything together. Through the use of your time, you change the way you do things. You must commit extra time with nearly every thing you do. For instance, when opening a piece of mail, take the extra time – right then and there - to handle that piece of mail all the way to its conclusion. Many times you merely take a quick glace at the envelope and then set it aside "to do" later. This only creates another job for you, and leads you to more clutter.

You also need to consider how much time you are willing to spend organizing. Take a moment and give this some genuine thought. If you are not willing to spend time on organizing, it won't happen. On the other hand, regularly committed time designated to organizing can lead to an organized home, office and life!

My most-recommended tip relating to "time" is, The 2 Minute Rule. If you can handle something in two minutes or less, do it immediately and be done with it. Is this always realistic? No. However, you need to have a starting place and something to strive for or you will procrastinate and never get started.

I love the quote, "The easiest way to get something done is to begin." I challenge YOU to begin today by committing, investing, and devoting time to organizing your life both at home and at work.

QUICK TIP: *Finish all projects completely before moving on to another. This includes putting away all tools and supplies used and cleaning the area where the project was worked on. This helps to eliminate the backsliding effect. Take an extra few moments now and you won't have to take a day later to catch up.*

Sherri Papich, Organize Your Life LLC, Springville, New York

Chapter 3

THE #1 ORGANIZING MYTH

"It is not always how it looks."

-Unknown

There is a standard misconception about exactly 'how' organization should look. For example, I have a client (we will call her Jane) who really struggled with this. I worked with Jane through a series of sessions over a period of several months. We focused on the paper and mail that seemed to always cover Jane's kitchen counter and dining room table.

Jane made huge progress. She was regularly using a calendar, she kept daily to-do lists, and her backlog of paper clutter had really dwindled.

When I came to Jane's house for another session and we walked into her dining room, Jane sighed with frustration. I dug deeper with some gentle probing questions. Eventually, I discovered that although Jane had a pretty good handle on her time management, and could now even find most things, she was deeply bothered by the stacks of paper and items on her dining room table. Jane had been fooled by the myth that organized equals neat.

Jane's visual perception of organization equated to a showcase home. Similar to what you might see on daytime television.

I am going to let you in on a secret, and it's a big one. The folks on daytime television don't receive mail and their "pretend" kids don't bring home backpacks full of stuff either!

The definition of being "organized" is being able to find what you want when you need it. This means it does not necessarily have to be neat. As long as you can find it, you are considered organized. It's that simple.

On the other hand, you can also be organized and neat. Like much of organization, this is really just a personal preference. The point to be made is that organization and neatness do not necessarily have to go hand-in-hand.

Once I filled Jane in on the real truth about organizing and neatness, she was happily relieved. Plus, Jane needed to realize that her table was covered with stuff because this was her staging area for doing all of her daily projects and tasks. So, I gave Jane a few options. The first option was that Jane could continue to use her table as a workspace 24/7. Another option for Jane was to use the space during the day, but remove her work for mealtimes. Finally, the third option would be that Jane could find another area for her workspace. While the first option may have been the most convenient, the latter two reflected less clutter. The final decision was ultimately up to Jane. If (or when) the clutter became too much, Jane could actually choose to change directions and opt for one of the latter less-cluttered options. The last time I was at Jane's, she was still using the table for her staging area. Jane has chosen organized over neat - and that's just fine!

QUICK TIP: People often think "It takes so much time!" Remember the title of this book? Set a timer for 2 minutes a day and tackle one area of your home that's bothering you. In the long run, the time you set aside to get organized will more than pay off!

Sally Ficken
Cedar Rapids, Iowa

Chapter 4

THE TOP ORGANIZING SECRET
●●●

What is the secret answer to getting organized? The 'secret' to getting organized really comes down to four very simple steps.

1) Gather all like items together. This is the very first step in being able to find what you need when you need it. When you have similar items together, this eliminates having to look in two, three, or more different places for something. Additionally, when all like items are together, you can take a very quick inventory of the number of items on hand, as needed.

2) Containerize. Once you have your like items grouped together, "contain" those grouped items in a container of some form. Take a look at the

size of the grouping, consider the available space of where it is to be stored, and then purchase the container based on these variables. Quite often the step of purchasing containers is done before like items are grouped together. If this is the case, you are actually just guessing at the size and type of container needed. Buying a container before knowing what is really needed sometimes equates to trying to fit a square peg in a round hole. It's best to take the time to truly evaluate your needs, and then buy appropriately, and only, if needed.

Plastic totes are the first type of container that often comes to mind. However, think outside of the box and consider alternatives like crates, baskets, drawers, and boxes. Moreover, if you are looking to organize paperwork, then items such as file folders, expandable files, trays, file drawers, and cabinets need to be evaluated as viable options. You can check out more specific information on containers in Chapter 11.

3) Label, label, label. Once the items have been grouped together and contained, the next step is to label the contained items. Even if it is a clear tote, and you think you can see through it, label it! Seeing through the container when you are in a hurry is actually not as easy or efficient as you might think.

Several years ago, I cleaned out and cleared out our holiday decorations. I bought new clear see-through totes and stored my favorite decorations in them. I had each tote separated by colors of décor. For instance, one tote had all of our blue and silver tree decorations, another tote contained all of our gold and burgundy decorations, and yet another had all of our green and red decorations. Keep in mind that this was back when I wasn't totally sold on the idea of labeling. I figured that I knew what was in each tote, and heck, they were see-through! I sincerely didn't see any real good reason for labeling them.

Well, eleven months later, I went to retrieve my nicely organized holiday decorations. I found that I couldn't see-through the totes well enough to determine which décor was in what tote. I spent quite some time pulling down the totes from the shelves, opening each one, reshuffling them, and greatly confusing myself in the process. Needless to say, I quickly grabbed a label and a marker to appropriately label each of the totes in a manner that indicated what the specific contents were.

The added bonus to labeling items is that not only will you, or someone else, be able to find an item, but it will also be exponentially easier to know where an item is supposed to be returned to. Imagine how helpful it would be if your kids and/or spouse were able to return things to their proper home. Can you 'feel' the value of organization yet?

Yes, I know you might be thinking, "Wow, I really need to label every container?" While labeling every container might be helpful, there will be times when it just does not make sense. For instance, our kitchen cabinets act as containers, but labeling the cabinet with the dishes probably does not make much sense. So, use your best judgment in those types of instances. However, be certain to recognize the overall rule and label any and every time it makes sense to do so.

4) Create a home for everything and keep it in its home. Yes, every contained and labeled item needs a designated home. In addition, each item needs to always be in its home when not in use. Remember your mom saying, "Put it away?" Putting it away is simply putting it in its designated home.

I can guarantee that if you follow these four basic steps, you will have the 'secret' to getting (and more importantly) staying organized. It all comes down to being able to find what you need, when you need it.

QUICK TIP: *Feeling overwhelmed by organizing a large room? Focus on ONE area in that room, such as a bookcase or closet area. Gradually move around that room organizing, as your time permits, until the whole room is completed!*

Gaylynn Winn, Organize it...One Room at a Time, Columbia, Missouri

Chapter 5

THE DAILY GRIND:
MAIL AND PAPERWORK

"Leaving things scattered around the house is a surefire way to lose them."

-MarthaStewart.com

Grand Central Station is one of New York City's most famous landmarks. It's also a very busy hub of activity, serving nearly 575,000 visitors a day. Kitchens are essentially the Grand Central Station of most homes in America.

Multiple meals and snacks are prepared in your kitchen day-in and day-out. Because of this, it is absolutely critical that your kitchen is well functioning. Appliances, dishes, food, utensils- and the dreaded plastic ware and their lids - all need well thought-out designated homes of storage.

The kitchen is also notoriously known as the most popular dumping ground for papers, mail, and every other item as it first enters the household. With the rapid rate of paper generation in our world today, it is extremely easy to become overwhelmed with papers and mail. This can happen in as little as one week! Because of this, it is important to have a paper processing system in place to help you keep up.

Carve out a mini-office in a niche somewhere in the kitchen. It is actually quite common to process the mail and papers in the kitchen, and then *transfer all of* the paper to the home office. Unfortunately, because of our fast-paced society, we simply don't have time to walk down the hallway, upstairs, or downstairs to file away papers in the home office. Plus, it simply is not convenient to do so. Instead, many of us create piles on the kitchen table, or counters, and then we play the "moving stacks of paper" game. Heaven forbid someone should come for a visit! That's when we do the "sweep the papers into a box and stash them in the closet" game. All along we continually convince ourselves we will magically get to all of that paper… later!

If you want a system that is more likely to succeed, based on the fact that you are more likely to use it, set up a mail processing system that is simple to use.

Create a file center that includes file folders labeled with the various common categories of papers that come into your household. Store the file folders in alphabetical order and place them in an accessible location such as on your countertop or in a cabinet. Ideally, you want this process to be as simple as opening a cabinet door and dropping a paper into the appropriate file folder. Then, as those files fill up, go through them and move only the long-term items to your home office. Utilizing this process means you only need to "file" papers away in your home office a couple times a year - versus everyday! That makes for fewer trips down the hallway, upstairs, or downstairs!

Rethinking the way you use the space you have, and making that space work for you, is a simple solution to successfully managing your daily mail and paper. Soon, processing the mail in the kitchen and moving it to its filing system will be a thing of the past – you will have moved the filing system to the mail!

QUICK TIP: Have your recycle bin, letter opener and mail center together preferably near your door. That way, you can process your mail before it gets further than your hallway.

**Zele Avradopoulos, Zorganize,
Waltham, Massachusetts**

Chapter 6

HELP, STICKY NOTES EVERYWHERE!

•••

If you are the queen - or king - of sticky notes, listen up! Sticky notes can be a great organizing tool when used the correct way. However, using your sticky notes to keep track of telephone conversations, lists of items to complete, or important information may not be the best use of this popular office staple.

The challenges with sticky notes are twofold: they stick to the wrong thing or they simply don't stick at all. The chance of losing, or accidently misplacing, a sticky note is great. Sticky notes, therefore, are not recommended for everyday standard note taking by any means. You can eliminate the sticky notes, and the scratch paper, by using something just a little bit more permanent. Instead, challenge yourself to jot down all of your telephone messages and notes in a simple spiral notebook. Spiral notebooks work really great because of their durability and permanency. There are a variety of spiral notebook sizes available. Choose one that meets your needs. If you find that you truly cannot break the habit of grabbing a sticky note or scratch piece of paper, that's okay. Grab yourself a spiral notebook anyway, and then tape your notes into the notebook. Voila! You now have all of your notes in one much more permanent place.

An obvious benefit of eliminating the sticky notes, or moving them into a notebook, is the reduction in visual clutter. By removing this visual clutter, your mind will be less stressed and better able to focus. Try it, you might like it!

Does this mean you have to ban sticky notes from your home and office? Of course not! Sticky notes are actually helpful in a couple of different ways. For one, they come in all different colors and sizes. Personally, I love the super sticky notes that are lined and available in an array of bright colors. I use these particular notes, sparingly, for those all-important notes that I need to keep front and center. Their super stickiness really helps keep them in place so they can serve their actual purpose.

I also find sticky notes are great for helping to jog the memory. By slapping a note on top of a group of related papers and writing down a checklist of things to complete for that particular project, you can simply check off the items as you complete them. The added bonus is that if you are interrupted in the project, the checklist steers you quickly back to where you left off.

QUICK TIP: *Keep a notebook with you and remember to also put one next to your bed so you won't forget any great ideas.*

Joetta Tucker, My Organizing Friend,
Geneva, New York

Chapter 7

SOS! IT'S TAX TIME

"Tracking invoices and receipts is an essential task—not only for your own record keeping but also for the IRS."

-Joshua Zerkel, owner Custom Living Solutions

You know the saying, "There are two things that are certain, death and taxes." Although taxes come around every year, many people still find it an excruciating process. The best way to get a handle on this is to set up a system for tracking and maintaining all of your tax information and documents. If you do not have a system in place and tax season is right around the corner, it is not too late. You can still get a handle on it.

To begin, start digging through the papers, piles, boxes, and cabinets. You are looking for anything that says "Important Tax Document Enclosed," or "Retain Receipt for Tax Purposes." You are also looking for anything that refers to the appropriate tax year.

There are some specific categories of documents you may need for preparing your tax return. Although not all-inclusive, some examples of documents you might need include:

1099s: 1099 Interest, 1099 Dividends, and K-1s.

Capital Gains/Losses: Trade confirmations, spin-offs, and mergers.

Charitable Miles: Documentation of all charitable miles.

Child/Dependent Care: Receipts for child and/or dependent care.

Schooling: College savings plans and tuition paid.

Donations – Cash: Receipts for tax-deductible cash donations to churches, schools, and 501c (3) organizations.

Donations – Noncash: Receipts for tax-deductible noncash/in-kind donations to churches, schools, Goodwill, Salvation Army, and 501c(3) organizations.

Medical Bills: Explanation of benefits, statements, or invoices.

Mortgage Interest: Receipt(s) for tax-deductible mortgage interest.

Real Estate Taxes: Receipt(s) for tax-deductible property taxes.

Vehicle Registration Fees: Receipt for payment of tax-deductible vehicle registration fees.

W-2 Wage & Tax Statements: W-2s, 1099 income, disability payments, alimony, and state refunds.

Gather up all of these documents and sort them into the categories identified above. Much of your tax information arrives in your mailbox early in February. However, receipts and other documentation can be generated throughout the entire year.

To save you a great deal of digging and anxiety in future tax years, grab a big manila envelope right now and designate it as the official home for tax receipts and supporting documentation. Label it "Tax Info for 20XX" and add to it throughout the year as you acquire receipts. If you integrate this system now, you will be feeling pretty good when next tax season rolls around.

> **QUICK TIP:** *For the filing challenged, create a fun, inspiring category. For instance, instead of 401k, stocks, etc. call it Wealth. It's much more empowering.*
>
> ***Karen Flagg, Organize This! LLC,***
> ***Austin, Texas***

Chapter 8

MAGAZINE MADNESS

"There are only about six original ideas in the world and magazine editors keep rotating them – they just change the photos to make you think it's something new!"

-Peter Walsh, <u>It's All Too Much</u>

Reading clutter…we all have it. There is so much information in the world and much of it ends up on our kitchen table, in the magazine rack, next to the bed or shoved under the sofa. So, why don't you just pitch it? Well, of course, there must be something of extreme importance in it. It is also the fear of throwing out the unknown…not knowing exactly what it is you are actually pitching.

When it comes to "letting go," your emotional decision-making skills kick into high gear. To manage this, you need to think beyond the emotions and move into some logical decision-making.

Let's take magazines for example. If you have a backlog of 10 magazines, that doesn't seem like many. However, if the magazines arrive on a monthly basis, that is almost one year of magazines in arrears. Also, when you take into account that it takes a good two hours to read a magazine from cover to cover, that is 20 hours of reading for a backlog of 10 magazines. Twenty hours! Think about it, that is almost one full day or half of a workweek. Logically, now what were just 10 magazines is now half of a workweek.

Expectations are another component of reading clutter. People quite often set unrealistically high expectations of themselves. Get real. Are you really going to spend what equates to half a workweek getting caught up on reading materials?

So, how do you combat the reading clutter for good?

BE CONSISTENT. Have a system in place for giving attention to your magazines. For example, take 20 minutes at the end of each day to wind down and read; or take the time in the morning to ease into your day by reading before things get busy.

BE SYSTEMATIC. Replace the old magazine with the new one as soon as it arrives.

BE REALISTIC. Logically evaluate the time you "really" have to read, not the time you "wish" you had to read.

BE AGGRESSIVE. Don't be afraid to tear out articles and information of importance. One or two articles occupy much less space than an entire magazine. Take care to file away the articles you do keep, so you can find them later. Better yet, scan them in to your computer and then pitch the paper all together.

BE CONSCIENTIOUS. Recycle the reading clutter in a recycling bin. Another option for recycling current materials would be to donate it to hospitals, doctor offices, or care centers. This goes for books, too. Once you have read a book, donate or sell it. A read book taking up space in your home, or office, is a thief of your space and energy!

QUICK TIP: Organizing is more about making decisions than it is about removing clutter. Determine how each item of yours makes you feel, and then you can make informed decisions about whether you really need it in your space or life. Once you start making these decisions you will gain more confidence and feel great.

Maggie Knack, A Knack for Organizing,
Edina, Minnesota

Chapter 9

LAUNDRY: THE SPIN CYCLE!

●●●

Laundry is one of those insurmountable chores. As you get one pile done, another pile surfaces. You cannot ignore the chore either, unless you want hygiene to be an issue for your family.

Like anything else, systems and streamlining relieves some of the never-ending stress. Let me share with you five tips to lighten your laundry work load.

1) Utilize hampers. There are three common options for containing and holding the dirty laundry: 1) individual hampers in each household member's bedroom; 2) community hamper for the entire household; or 3) separate sorting bins in the laundry room itself.

If space allows, separate bins in the laundry room is ideal. Separating like-items on the front end often elicits a savings of both time and space. Separate sorting bins may include: whites, colors, darks, towels, reds, khakis, and special care. Special care holds hand-washing, delicate cycle, or dry cleaning items.

2) Mesh bags. If you dread matching clean white socks, this tip is for you. Assign each family member their own mesh bag for collecting their dirty white socks. Toss the mesh bag and all contents into the washer and then the dryer. When the cycle is complete, match up is easy. You will only be matching up socks from within each bag, so this can be the difference between matching 20 socks versus 80 socks.

3) Hang or fold immediately. When the dryer stops remove your clothing immediately. Hang or fold all of the items. Tossing them into a basket is just creating another job for you. Plus, an added benefit of folding, or hanging, right away is that you stave off wrinkles.

4) Only start what time allows. Before throwing in a load of laundry, make sure you have time to complete the process. This includes time to transfer the load, remove it from the dryer, and then fold or hang the items. It is a waste of resources, not to mention odorous, if you must re-wash your laundry because you did not get the load transferred before the mildew smell set in.

5) Share the responsibility. Do not hesitate to involve the entire family in the process. Laundry is a life skill everyone should know. This is a great opportunity to give each family member their own mesh bag of socks to match. Many hands do make light work.

Implementing any one or more of these tips will help with the never-ending laundry battle. So, go ahead, try one out and lighten your load.

QUICK TIP: Put things where you use them. For example, if your laundry room is on the same floor as your bedroom put a hook near the dryer and laundry bin. I get ready for morning by putting my outfit on the hook. In the winter, a few minutes before bedtime, I put my nightgown in the dryer so it is toasty warm. I drop my dirty clothes in the laundry basket because it is right there. In the morning, my clothes are already there waiting for me and the hook is now free for my night clothes.

Rie Brosco, RieOrganize!,
Philadelphia, Pennsylvania

Chapter 10

ORGANIZING: ALL WORK, NO PLAY?

•••

One of the most important tips and strategies for maintaining organization involves setting up a system that is user-friendly. It needs to be convenient. If it is too difficult to do, or if it demands too many steps, you will not do it.

Three Barriers Keeping You from Being Organized

1) **Inconvenience of locating files.** I would venture to guess that within the multitude of papers on your kitchen counter, a chunk of them just need to be filed. You probably looked at each piece of paper and did the "put it in a pile to file later" move we all know so well.

Does this scenario sound familiar? You open the mail and deal with the paperwork in the kitchen, but have your filing cabinet in the home office down the hallway, upstairs, or in the basement. If this is the case, filing is not convenient for you.

Your solution involves one of two options. You can either move your paperwork processing close to your file cabinet, or you can create a file system in your kitchen.

2) **Closed containers or boxes.** Storing items in closed containers or boxes does appear tidier. However, if your items only make it to the top of the container, or box lid, and do not get put away inside of the container, you have defeated your purpose.

Why don't you just put the items in the container or box? It comes down to convenience. Many times it boils down to simply taking too many steps to do so. In some instances, it may include a series of steps-- unlocking the lid, lifting it off, putting the item inside, closing the lid, and latching the lid. That is five steps.

Your solution comes down to something very simple--remove the lid (and keep it off). Now you can just drop your item in. That is one step versus five steps. Which would you rather do?

3) **Failure to create a home for all things.** I know you agree that if you put all things away where they belong, you will be able to find what you need when you need it. However, if you do not have a designated home for something, you will find it much easier to drop it on the counter or shove it in the closet.

How can you make sure things have a home and get put away? Simply said, you will need to get over the discomfort and inconvenience of making a decision. Clutter is simply the failure to make a decision. Discipline yourself to make a decision and act upon it. Focus on your self-talk and be sure to cheer yourself on.

QUICK TIP: Fasten a safety pin to the bottom right corner seam of your fitted sheets. This will save time and frustration trying to figure out the top and bottom from the sides each time you change the bed.

Betty Arnold, The Organizing Queen, Tampa, Florida

Chapter 11

CONTAINER INVASION

●●●

Do you have a closet or cupboard that is full of clutter? Many people do and don't know how to get it under control. One tool that is invaluable is the "container."

When you hear the word container, a plastic tub usually comes to mind. It is important to note that there are many different types of containers. From an organizing standpoint, "to contain" means to create some kind of boundary for like objects. It can be a physical boundary such as a plastic tub, basket, file folder, letter tray, etc. It can also be "contained" by an invisible boundary.

An example of an invisible boundary is, "I always leave my master list on the upper right hand corner of my desk." The master list isn't contained by any "physical boundary," but instead by an invisible boundary.

One obvious advantage of containers is the "neat" appearance it tends to provide. Moreover, with like things contained in each container, it becomes much easier to find the items you need. It will also lend itself to reduced duplication of items and save money.

Many times if something cannot be found, another of the same item is bought. This duplicates your time and money. Containers are one organization tool that can help to control the clutter.

While there is an entire arsenal of organizing products available on the market, there are several considerations to be made when selecting the right organizing tool. Before investing in an organizing product, or supply, it is important to know what you need before you buy it. On many occasions, those who are disorganized do not know how to "get organized," and will do anything to try to accomplish this aim. Usually, this means raiding the organizing aisle at the local home improvement store. The excitement and expectation is "once I get home and put these containers in place, I will get organized." This feeling is quickly deflated after getting home when everything does not become magically organized.

Organizing books are also a great tool; however, there is little chance you will learn from them if you never read them. The organizing book we see quite commonly at our many clients' homes is entitled, "How to Get Organized - When You Don't Have the Time." Ironically, every client we have asked about that book has replied, "I haven't had time to read it yet." Quite possibly an organizing book is not the right tool for everyone.

A colleague of mine and I regularly attend national professional organizing conferences. Along with the seminars and educational opportunities, there is a wide array of vendors. It is an opportunity for professional organizers to see and sample the many organizing products available. All of the newest and greatest products are on display.

At one of the vendor expos, the latest and greatest organizing product was a program to scan receipts into your computer so you can go "paperless" with all those pesky receipts that accumulate quickly. This cutting-edge technology was garnering quite a frenzy and many were magnetically attracted to it. I am sure the vendor was selling the idea as the best thing to come along since sliced bread. Remember, an organizing product is not "the right tool," unless we need it and use it.

I pondered on the thought of whether or not this might be the right organizing tool for some of our clients. After thinking it through, I realized most of our residential clients do not need to organize and electronically store their receipts. What they really need is some education on the limited number of receipts that need to be kept. Some hands-on training and coaching on letting-go of and purging all the unnecessary receipts would be beneficial. From a businesses perspective, this product may be the right tool, but for the average household it is likely not the best and most efficient use of either time or resources.

So, what is the right container or tool? It is whatever will help you reach your goal of becoming organized. For some it may be a tote or container. For others it may be the services of a professional organizer who can teach organizing skills and/or help determine what organizing products are needed in order to actually *get organized.*

QUICK TIP: *Use a CD organizer that straps to the visor in your car to hold your retail coupons; i.e. Bed, Bath & Beyond and other retail stores!*

**Dawna Hall, Organize ME!,
Portland, Maine**

Chapter 12

OFFICIAL DIAGNOSIS: SURFACE CLUTTER

*"Our kitchen countertops evolve into cluttered
storage spaces, leaving us little room for what
it's there for — cooking!"*

-ContainerStore.com

Surface clutter is those items that accumulate on the common surfaces of your home like the dining room table, the kitchen countertop, or the floor by the front door. The difference between surface clutter and regular clutter is that surface clutter has a clearly defined home. You know where this stuff goes; it just has not made its way there. Most often this is a result of a busy schedule with limited time to return items to their proper place. Regular clutter accumulates because you do not know where it goes. My favorite definition of regular clutter is simply the failure to make a decision on something.

When I was growing up my mother had one day each week she devoted to cleaning and organizing the house. For her it was Thursday, as it was her day off work. Today's schedules are more hectic; there is more stuff. Face it; you don't have an entire day each week to devote to maintaining your house.

A while back we instituted a new system in our house referred to as the "whole house pick up."

Each week, generally on Saturdays because that fits our schedule, I announce a whole house pick up. I warn you, I often get moaning and eye rolling from my kids, and sometimes my spouse. However, when it is finished, it is all worth it.

Here is how "whole house pick up" works:
Standing in the kitchen, I corral the troops. I pick up one item of surface clutter. I then hand it to a family member, direct them to put it away, and send them off. As soon as they are done with that one task, they immediately return to the kitchen for another item to put away. We continue this process moving to other areas of the house until all surface clutter is put away.

Some things to consider when using this system:

1) Know your family's capabilities. Give simpler and easier tasks to younger kids. Give more

complex, and maybe harder-to-reach tasks to older kids or to your spouse.

2) Have clearly designated homes for all items. Without this, you will be sending your family members on an expedition of finding, or creating, a place to shove things.

3) Give clear defined instructions of where items are to go.

4) Include your spouse in the system. He/she will expedite the process and the participation will be a good example of family teamwork.

5) Give out only one task at a time, instead of a handful of items going to different places. Too many tasks increase the chance of getting side tracked, or misplacing items.

The selfish incentive for this system is I do not do all the work by myself. More importantly, however, my kids are learning that maintaining a household is important. They learn we can work together as a team and accomplish so much more in less time. As a reward for our kids' participation, they are able to do something they enjoy later in the day, plus (as everyone knows) "when momma's happy everyone's happy."

QUICK TIP: Make your entryway an organization zone. Have a place for keys, mail, and backpacks. Get a bench with cubbies or a hall tree with hooks for a simple way to unload the day in an organized way.

Lisa Tella, Neat Chic Organizing, Ballwin, Missouri

Chapter 13

TURN OVER A NEW SPRING LEAF

●●●

"It's the perfect time to embrace the Feng Shui art of uncluttered living."

-LifeOrganizers.com

Spring is one of my favorite times of the year. The days become longer, the flowers start budding, and the trees turn green. Spring is the time to turn over a new leaf. It's also the perfect time to de-clutter from the winter, clean up, and clear out.

By adhering to a few simple steps, you can have your home and life ready for a better season.

1) Out with the old. Sift through last season's clothes and get rid of those items you did not wear, do not like, or do not fit anymore. Limit your wardrobe to only one "fantasy size" of clothes!"

Clear out the expired medicines, as well as outdated food in the cabinets and in the refrigerator.

2) Top to bottom. Begin each cleaning project by systematically starting at the top and moving to the bottom. Dust falls down so take advantage of gravity. Start with the ceiling fans, move down the walls with a dry swiffer, and vacuum last.

3) One project at a time. This is the most efficient way to spring clean. Following this method will lead to completed projects rather than numerous projects started and none finished. Plus, completing a single project will provide a sense of accomplishment and motivation to keep cleaning and organizing.

4) Gather a cleaning kit. Inventory and stock up on the cleaning products you will need. Minimize the number of products on hand. Don't waste your time and energy buying a dozen different cleaners. Keep it simple. The essential quick-cleaning kit includes: disinfectant, glass cleaner, furniture polish, rubber gloves, toilet bowl cleaner, sponges, and a multi-purpose cleaner. Put your kit in a caddy with a handle and you are ready to go.

5) Don't over do it. Instead of doing marathon cleaning and organizing, make a schedule and attack one job every couple of days. Save big jobs, like the garage, for a nice full day and do inside jobs on rainy days.

6) Heavy-duty shower cleaning. Cleaning the shower is probably one of the most dreaded spring-cleaning jobs. If you are looking for new options and ideas, some products you might consider are: Mr. Clean Magic Eraser ®, Black & Decker Scrubber ®, and The Works ® Cleaner. I have found all these products to be beneficial.

7) Power of the dishwasher. Don't overlook utilizing your dishwasher. It's a simple way to clean the greasy aluminum filters from above the stove, stove-top grills, grill grates, organizer caddies from the shower, non-delicate light fixtures, and plastic drawer organizers.

Take the time to turn a new spring leaf, shed the winter clutter, and enjoy the warmer weather!

QUICK TIP: *When you have an old washing machine or dryer to get rid of, call your local waste management company and they might come and pick it for a minimal fee CURBSIDE!!*

MaSanda LaRa Gadd, HeartVisions,
Bothell, Washington

Chapter 14

WHAT IS IT ABOUT SHOPPING?

*"It is up to us to know that we are being
conditioned to buy as many things as possible.
Even the layout of a supermarket is planned
in detail, set up so that you have to pass as
many 'optional' items as possible."*

**-Judi Culbertson and Marj Decker,
<u>Scaling Down</u>**

There are many people who like to shop, even
when there isn't anything in particular that is
needed. It's fun to share shopping time with friends
and family, check out new stores, or the new
seasonal items. For many, it's also such an
accomplishment to find that "good deal." Shoppers
often like to calculate how much they "saved," and
share the excitement with family at home. Often
times, family will respond with an "oh,"

accompanied, sometimes, with a look that seems a little glazed over.

I, too, on occasion participate in directionless shopping with friends. It's a social outing. However, I realize the importance of evaluating the needs and the purpose of the items purchased. I have had perfectionism "hang up" since childhood– especially with clothes. This leaves me with a dismal wardrobe, at times. However, I have discovered it is "okay" to be choosy.

During your next shopping venture, ask yourself a few simple questions before you buy:

1) Where will this go, when I get home?
2) Should something else leave the closet to make room for it?
3) If this is a project, do I have time for it?
4) Will this add value to my life?

How do you feel when you look at your unused items? The stress of keeping track of items, finding them, or even feeling guilty, isn't a healthy addition to your life. Keeping life a little simpler takes thought – developing the habit of a conscience thinking process – definitely adds value to your life. Like any good habit, it takes practice to form this new way of thinking.

People too often end up with closets, boxes in the attic, and tubs in the basement, all full of items they no longer use. By being more critical in the shopping process, you will bring home only the things you really love, have space for, and will actually use.

Immerse yourself in the "social" aspect of shopping time with friends and family. Develop a thinking process, and ask yourself critical questions before you buy. Every item you bring home should be useful, whether for practical purposes, or aesthetic enjoyment. If it may potentially cause dilemma, or stress, admire it in the store, show it to your co-shoppers, and leave it there. You just saved money and stress!

QUICK TIP: *Don't succumb to large quantity purchasing simply because it's a good deal. Purchase in quantity only when you have space for that item.*

Brenda McElroy, Organized By Choice, Fresno, California

Chapter 15

HELP ME! I CAN'T LET GO
●●●

*"Keeping too much stuff causes you
unnecessary stress every time you look at
the clutter while wishing it wasn't there."*

-*Patty Kreamer, <u>But I Might Need It Someday</u>*

Letting go is a barrier for most people. For some, understanding the skill of how to process the items is all that is needed. For many others, it's the psychological hurdle of letting go that brings the biggest challenge. This chapter will outline both the system for letting go, as well as things to consider that may help you overcome the psychological attachment you have to your "stuff."

What is S-WEE-P™?

S-sort, WEE-weed and P-purge represents the formula needed to reduce and reorganize the clutter in your home. Let's talk about the procedure for completing this simple three-step process. I will use, as an example, a bathroom closet.

S-Sort: In order to start any organizing project, it is critical that all items are initially sorted. Sort the items into like-item categories. In other words, as you start pulling items out of our bathroom closet, group the items together into categories such as shampoo, conditioner, soap, toothpaste, toothbrushes, brushes, combs, hair accessories, bath gels, etc. Depending on the number of items in each group, it may make sense to combine some groups together. If you have only one shampoo and conditioner, you can put those together in one group. Likewise, grouping combs and brushes together may be appropriate based on quantity.

W-Weed: Weeding is traditionally implemented at two different times. The first occurs as you pull items out of the closet in the sorting process. For instance, if you pull out a shampoo bottle that is empty, weeding it out at this point is appropriate. In other words, you do not put obvious items to be disposed of into the sorting categories for later. Obvious items are those that don't work, are broken, gross, non-functioning, or items you readily know you don't like or need.

The second opportunity for weeding is after all items have been sorted into categories. It is at this point you compare and contrast all of the items within each category. For example, you may have six tubes of toothpaste. One tube is a flavor no one in the household likes, so weed it out here. Another tube dispenses funny and makes a mess, weed it out now. A third tube, discovered way in the back of the closet, is of questionable quality and hence should be weeded out now as well.

P-Purge: Purging is the process of determining where the "weeded" items go, and the actual releasing of those weeded items. Common choices are trash, recycle, give away, sell, and keep - but store in another location. A box, or bag, is needed for each of these categories. As the items are purged, immediately deal with and handle the purged categories. In other words, take the trash bag to the garage, likewise with the recycling. Make arrangements for, and deliver, items that are to be given away. Do the same with items to sell. Immediately take items to be kept, but stored elsewhere, to their new and more appropriate home.

After the **S-WEE-P** ™ process, you are left with "keep" items needing to go back into your bathroom closet. Once you have your "keep" categories identified, then containerize, label, and place those organized, containerized, labeled categories back in your closet. Step back, enjoy the clutter-free look, and share your accomplishment with your family and friends!

Time and Energy Bandits

According to Xplor International, the amount of paper printed in the world more than doubled from 1995 to 2005. Marketing campaigns for buying "stuff" get more and more creative, items are made for use and disposal, and accessibility from the Internet and discount stores continues to rise. All of this makes it way too easy for our lives to be overcome with "stuff."

It is important to consciously recognize that every item brought into your household is a thief of your time and energy.

So, how do you rid yourself of "stuff?"

There are two opportunities for doing this. One is letting go; and two, is prevention.

Letting Go. This process isn't easy for many people largely because most decisions are based on emotion. For sentimental items, you may fear that letting go of the item will be a letting go of the memory. Once you realize your memories are in your heart, and in your mind, letting go of the item is much easier. At that point such item is defined as only a thing, not a memory.

Many others have a difficult time letting go of something that still has "life" in it. In other words, they justify a perceived way the item could be used or could potentially come in handy later on. Emotion is what tells you the 35 butter containers in your cabinet are still in perfect shape, and letting them go would be a shame. Does that sound familiar? It makes perfect sense from an emotional standpoint, but logically, it's a waste of space as well as a thief of your time and energy. Think about it, a butter container isn't really alive, so it can't have any "life left in it."

Prevention. There are many necessary papers that come into your home via the mail. Add to that the necessary items, products, and food you need to live and you have enough to keep you busy 24/7. You may have little control over these necessary things, but what about those items you invite and bring into your home? Here's where you can focus on prevention:

Before you place anything in your shopping cart or order something online, apply the "Value Test." Ask yourself if this item is going to add value to your life. If so, how? Take this test one step further and determine if you could legitimately "sell your need" for this item to your spouse, or a friend. In the alternative, simply talk to yourself out loud about it.

Let me tell you a story of a client who realized the benefit of saying things out loud. We will call her Jennifer. I was hired to help Jennifer and her husband weed through and purge boxes and boxes of paper they had accumulated. We were in the sorting process and I kept finding church bulletins with notes on them. I had quite a pile of them after just a few minutes. I took a moment and asked Jennifer about the bulletins. "So Jennifer, tell me about the bulletins. It looks like notes you have taken, maybe from the sermons? What do you do with them? Do you go back and look at them?" Jennifer's response was priceless. She discovered the power of verbalizing her so-called needs. Jennifer said, "You know when I say it in my mind it makes perfect sense, but when I say it out loud it sounds stupid. I don't need to keep these." With that, she promptly scooped up the pile of church bulletins and tossed them in the recycling.

What happened here? By my evaluation, Jennifer's expectations were set too high. Although Jennifer had good intentions of going back to her notes, she knew realistically that was never going to happen. By saying it out loud, or in this case, just thinking about saying it out loud, the light bulb went on. Jennifer had an ah-ha moment, and she was okay with letting the bulletins go.

In the alternative, if Jennifer had referenced her notes on a regular basis, or if she had a specific plan for using them, they would have been kept in an organized manner so she could find them later.

It's so easy to convince yourself and justify things in your mind that saying it out loud is sometimes all it takes for you to realize your "need" is based on "emotion" rather than "logic."

System for Weeding Out

As you go through the weeding out process, there are basically four choices for the ultimate destination of your stuff. They are as follows:

1) **Pitch it or Recycle it.** If it is something that has no value, no one else would want it, or it can't be sold, then pitch it or recycle it. Preserve our environment whenever possible and recycle. Check with your local government about recycling options in your area. Also, take care to shred all items containing personal information.

   An alternative to keeping items out of the landfill is something called Freecycle. The Freecycle network is a worldwide effort to share items for free among members. Membership is free and the goal is to share items so they are kept out of the trash. For more information go to www.freecycle.org.

2) **Give it Away.** Donate to various charities like Goodwill or Salvation Army and secure a tax write off. This is a perfect option for those items with little monetary value and not worth selling. For something to be worth selling, it needs to have significant monetary value. Typical household items do not usually have significant value.

Both Goodwill and the Salvation Army have donation sites located throughout the entire U.S. Refer to the yellow pages in the phone book for specific locations. Or access their websites: Goodwill.com or SalvationArmyUSA.org.

3) **Sell it!** You will discover many items you no longer need that *do* have monetary value. There are numerous options for selling these items. Have a garage sale, take it to a consignment store, sell it on the Internet, have an auction, or an estate sale.

Refer to chapter 16 for more details on selling your items.

4) **Keep It!** Some of the items you come across will need to be kept. The items you keep will need to have the four organizing techniques applied. Refer to Chapter 4 for those four organizing techniques.

Essential Questions: Ask Yourself

There are a series of questions you will need to ask yourself as you weed through your items:
- Have I referred to it or used it in the last year?
- Do I have specific plans to use it in the future?
- Do I need to keep it for tax or legal reasons?
- Does it add value to my life?
- Can I easily replace it?
- What is the worst thing to happen if I get rid of it?

If you haven't used it in the last year, you don't have plans to use it, and you don't need it for tax or legal reasons, then it is probably "okay" to let it go.

Finally, ask yourself "what is the worst thing to happen if you let it go, and then you find you later need it." If you have to, close your eyes and imagine this scenario. What do you do? Can you borrow it from someone else? Can you easily buy another one? If you can live with either of these options, then toss it.

The purpose of these questions is to get you to start thinking logically about your stuff rather than emotionally.

Six Steps to Reduce Your Stuff

Sadly, many lives are overrun and overwhelmed with too much stuff. While this is not a surprise to many people, how to do something about "the stuff" is a struggle. To get you started, I have outlined six simple steps to really get you going down the right track.

1) Identify what you have and how much. You cannot just toss something out because you have the relentless fear of throwing out something valuable or important. Therefore, you must sort your like-items together into different piles. This process will allow you to determine exactly what you have and how much of each you have.

2) Decide what and how much you really need. Now that you have completed Step 1, you are ready to make an informed decision about narrowing down your keepers. For example, if you discover you have nine steak knife sets (and you never entertain) letting go of seven sets is pretty easy. This is where you choose your favorites and let go of the inferior quality items.

3) Step outside your body. Mentally pretend to be someone else helping you go through your stuff. It may seem a bit wacky, but talk to yourself out loud about reasons for keeping things. Often times you can justify things in your mind, but if speaking them out loud is not convincing to yourself then it probably means you are hanging onto clutter. Do not hesitate to be ruthless with yourself.

4) Become a more discriminating shopper. Avoid impulse buying. If you find something you think you have to have, apply the 24-hour rule. Wait 24 hours and if you still think you need it, go buy it. Chances are you will not feel the need for it after the waiting period.

5) Declare your home at maximum capacity. I declared that our home had reached maximum capacity a few years ago. If we continued to add more stuff to our household, I was quite sure I was going to go over the edge. To ensure our capacity does not increase, we utilize the one-in/one-out rule. This means before something new can come in, something current must go out. Like all rules, stand behind them 100% strong, or they won't work.

6) Toss it in a dated box. An easy test to see if you really need something is to toss it in a box with a destroy date, make the destroy date six or nine months out. Make a deal with yourself: if you have not used anything in the box by the destroy date, dump the box without looking in it. With the passage of time, it's unlikely you will miss it.

A Holiday for Letting Go

If you find it difficult to motivate yourself to let things go, you may want to start out with baby steps. There is a day each year dedicated to letting go. June 23 is "Let It Go" day. Mark it on your calendar now and take the day to let a few things go.

If you did any spring cleaning and organizing you probably spied a few things in your home that needed to go. If those items are still sitting in a box or shoved in a corner when June 23 comes around, take advantage of the holiday and move those things out of your home.

Often times, items you want to get rid of hang around simply because you are not sure what to do with them. To make the "Letting Go" easier, I have assembled a listing of options for your gently loved items.

Clothing: Garage sale
                   Consignment store
                   Favorite charity

Magazines: Hospitals
                   Doctor or dentist offices

Retirement homes

Books:	Garage sale
	Libraries
	Schools
	Churches
Bedding/Towels:	Homeless shelters
	Animal shelters
	Humane societies
Eyeglasses:	Lions Club
	Optometrist offices
Building Materials:	Re-Store (www.habitat.org)
	High School shop departments
	Drama departments
*Computers:	Newspaper classifieds
	Schools
	Charities
	Landfill

*Be sure all data from computer hard drive is, or will be, erased.

Additionally, there is always the option to set an item out in front of your house by the road with a big "FREE" sign. Chances are, it will be grabbed up and treasured by a passerby. Your trash really may be someone else's treasure, but it can't be treasured until you "let it go."

QUICK TIP: *Finding a charity that is close to your heart might help you rid of excess easier. Local schools or nursing homes can usually use art supplies and/or books. Food pantries or shelters can use many necessities. Many organizations have yearly garage sales to benefit their cause and will accept just about anything that is clean and unbroken. If you are an animal lover, contact your local pet shelter to see what they will accept.*

Sherri Papich, Organize Your Life LLC, Springville, New York

Chapter 16

CAN I MAKE $$$ FROM MY STUFF?

"The main reasons you'll want to sell things is to have money, have more space, or reduce the expense of having things".

-Frugal-Living-Freedom.com

The short answer is "yes" you can get money *for* stuff. But making money *from* your stuff is not as likely. The biggest misconception we run into with our clients is the thought that their stuff is more valuable than it really is. Many people think they should get back close to or as much money as they originally put into an item. I am going to let you in on a secret…most of the world doesn't find as much value in your stuff as you do. Also, purchasing household goods and clothing is *not* an investment. These items do not hold their original value. Most items depreciate, and there is actually a point in the life of items that they depreciate to where they have little to no value.

By using standard depreciation tables used by the insurance industry, everyday dishes depreciate at 20% each year. This means that after 5 years, your dishes are worth $0. Likewise, a shirt or blouse depreciates at 33.3% each year. Its value is $0 after 3 years. (Claimspages.com)

While there are rare items that hold or increase in value, the likelihood of this is minimal. With the birth of the Internet and www.ebay.com, you can do a simple search to find out if an item you own has any significant value.

For instance, I had a large hardback book about the John F. Kennedy family that I wanted to sell in a garage sale. However, I was not sure what to price it at or if maybe it had a collector's value. The original cost was about $40.00. Who knows, maybe this was one of those items you hear about that increased in value…maybe its worth $1,000.00??!!??. Okay, I really didn't think it was worth that much. However, maybe it held value and selling it on eBay might bring in more money than at a garage sale. I went onto eBay and discovered that the going price was $2.99. Since I wasn't going to make much money from it, I now knew that and accepted that I could maybe get a couple of dollars for it.

To determine the value of anything you own, simply go to www.ebay.com. Sign into your account. If you do not have an account, open one. It is free and simple to do. Click on "advanced search," type in the description of your item, and click on "completed listings." This will provide you with a listing of auctions that have closed. If you find your item in this listing, you can see how much someone in the world was willing to pay for an item just like, or similar to, your item. Pay attention to the colors of the costs in the Price column. If the cost is green, it means it sold for that amount. If the color is red, no one bid on it. Listen carefully…no one in the world wanted it! If your item's price is in red, it's probably a pretty good indication there's not many people out there that want it - nor is it a hidden treasure.

Besides eBay there are other options for getting some money out of your stuff. Another internet option is www.CraigsList.com.

Garage Sale Today!

Spring is often a signal for garage sales.

After the cold, snowfall ridden winter, many feel burdened from the winter weight. What better way to shed some weight than to get rid of some stuff in your house? Preparing for a garage sale can be a lot of work, but having a plan can make the task much easier. So grab an empty box, and let's go!

1) Go through each of your clothes closets, one-by-one, item-by-item. Pull out all items that no longer fit, you don't like, or need repair. Toss the items that are of good used quality into the box. If they need repairing, either repair it or toss it in the trash. Don't hang onto something "you might do when you get around to it." That's simply hanging onto clutter.

2) Go through each kitchen cupboard, item-by-item. Pull out all items you have not used in the past year, do not have immediate plans to use, or are duplicate items. Toss these items in your box. (If you need a bigger box, good for you, keep going!)

3) Repeat the same process with every other closet, cupboard, drawer, and pile shoved throughout your home. Don't forget the garage and basement.

4) Find a big empty spot in your home, grab some pricing tags, a pen, and start pricing each item. For easier pricing, simply affix a colored dot to each item with each different color representing a different price. For example, all green dots are 50 cents, all red dots are $1.00, and so on. (If using the dot system be sure to prominently display a sign at your sale that explains your dot system.)

Now it's time to tell the world you have some treasures for sale.

Classified ads are still a great market for advertising your sale. Be sure to allow plenty of time to design your ad and meet the publishing deadline. Since newspapers tend to charge by the number of words, take time to carefully create your ad to make the most impact with the least amount of words.

Checklist Day Before Garage Sale

1) Go to the bank and get enough petty cash to make change as needed.
2) Set up tables.
3) Set up clothes hanging rods.
4) Set items for sale on tables and clothes racks.
5) Gather plastic bags for customer purchases.
6) Erect yard signs.
7) Gather calculator and cash box.

Best of luck on your garage sale!

Take a Tax Write Off

Donating items to an appropriate charity can put money back in your pocket. In fact, there is a company called Money For Your Used Clothing that sells a book that guarantees to "save a minimum of $250 on your taxes using [their] book −

Guaranteed." They also offer audit protection. You can check them out at www.mfyuc.com.

So, how do the mechanics work for writing off donations and saving money on your taxes?

You simply need to identify which federal tax bracket applies to you. For instance, if you are in the 25% tax bracket, and donate $1000, you save $250 ($1000 x 25% = $250) in federal taxes. If you pay state income taxes, you likely save even more.

If you choose to go this route, it is important to understand the IRS has specific requirements for writing off in-kind donations. As the rules are constantly changing, be sure to educate yourself on the current laws. However as of this writing, if you have charitable donations of over $500, you must complete Form 8283 and attach it to your tax return. In order to complete this form, you will need to itemize your donated items, assign an original cost, assign a fair market value, and have a valid receipt among other things. If you have questions, contact an account, attorney, or other qualified professional.

In order to take advantage of a tax write off, you also must consider that you need to itemize deductions on your tax return. If you take a standard deduction rather than itemize deductions, taking a deduction for your donated items may not be an option.

To Consign or Not To Consign

Another viable option for getting money for your stuff is consignment. Consignment is where you present (or consign) your items to a second-hand retailer. When your items sell, you receive a percentage of the selling price. Some consignment stores offer a 50/50 split, while others may be 60/40 (60% to the consignment store and 40% to you).

Over the years we have heard many clients say, "I am not going to do consignment because they give you only 40%." While this may be true, the thought process might need to be revisited. The consignor store or consignor organizers takes a cut because they are the ones preparing your items, merchandising your items, paying rent, payroll, and taxes. They are also wooing in customers and spending tens of thousands of dollars to do everything they can to sell your items. Through their efforts, they are increasing the market pool for your items. Without them, you eliminate the consignment split, but you also greatly minimize your group of potential customers.

Are there better types of items to consign than others? From my experience, I do believe this to be true. Furniture, sports equipment, kid's clothes, and electronics (if current enough) are the items I think make most sense to consign. However, keep in mind they must be in good to excellent condition.

Men's clothing doesn't usually consign well, unless it is designer and in excellent condition. Women's clothing will do okay on consignment if it is top-of-the-line designer clothing. For instance, a designer sweater new at a cost of $80.00 may consign for $50.00. At a 60/40 split, you would get $20.00 for the sweater. For adult clothing to be successful at consigning, and for consignment stores to accept it, it usually must be an originally higher cost designer item and still in style.

On the flip side, if you buy most of your clothing at discount stores, and pay $30.00 for a sweater, consignment price might be $10.00. In that case, you get $4.00 (40%), while the store gets $6.00. Because the profit on items such as this is so minimal, many consignment shops will not take run-of-the-mill clothing items.

Evaluate Your Options

As you can see there are options for getting money for your stuff. Because each item is different, you will need to evaluate it to determine which route makes sense for you. Will it be garage sale, donation, or consignment? The choice is yours.

If you are still not sure, contact a local professional organizer. They usually have a pulse on all the options in your area and can advise you on your best choices based upon your specific items.

> **QUICK TIP:** *The secret to a successful yard sale is foot traffic. The more folks who walk through your sale, the more you'll sell.*
>
> ***OrganizedHome.com***

Chapter 17

GARAGE DISASTERS!

"The biggest reason people struggle with garage organization is not because they can't do it, but because they are overwhelmed and don't know where to start."

-*Barry Izsak, author of*
<u>*Organize Your Garage in No Time*</u>

After every winter in the mid-west, my garage craves a makeover. The harsh sand, snow, and salt have done it in. While early spring is a perfect time to clear out and clean up, this activity can be done anytime of the year.

This job is best attacked when you can devote an entire day to it - or at the least, three-to-four hours. Gather the troops and distribute the brooms, rags and latex gloves. Yes, I said gather the troops. Cleaning out the garage is a big job and generally requires several sets of hands.

Begin by clearing everything out of the garage. After backing out all motorized vehicles, move out the other large items such as bicycles, wagons, lawnmowers, and so forth. Take care to sort items as you pull them out of the garage.

Remember the 'Organizing Secret' from Chapter 4:
1) Group like items together
2) Contain each group of like items
3) Label contained items
4) Create a home for everything and everything in its home

Continue to remove each and every item, box, and bag, and so on while carefully sorting the items into like groups on the driveway or lawn. Take care to throw away or recycle those items that are truly trash or do not work. Grab an empty box and label it "give away." In this box, you will toss items you no longer need, want, or have any plans to use. Be ruthless!

Once the garage is emptied, do some serious sweeping, scrubbing, and hosing. This may sound like a great deal of work and it's probably, as my kids would say, gross, but you will *love* how wonderfully fantastic you will feel once your garage is cleaned up.

Now it's time to move the "keepers" back into the garage while respecting Rules 2, 3, and 4 of the "Organizing Secret" above. Concentrate on keeping things stored up and off the floor, as it makes maneuvering about the garage much easier.

After your garage is all cleared out and cleaned up, do not stop there. Your job is not done! Grab your "give away" box and deliver it to your favorite charity.

Pat yourself on the back for getting your garage cleaned out and organized, as well as helping others by donating your unused items.

Now jump in the shower and enjoy the rest of your day!

QUICK TIP: *Keep an extra plastic grocery bag in your vehicle to use for trash. For even more convenience, put a bag holder in your garage.*

Joetta Tucker, My Organizing Friend
Geneva, New York

Chapter 18

IT'S TRAVEL TIME –BON VOYAGE
•••

Many of you have a trip planned at some point during the year. You may drive, you may cruise, you may fly, or you might participate in any combination of the three. The transportation choices are varied. No matter which mode of transportation you choose, you want it to be as pleasurable as possible. Arming yourself with some organizing travel tips and taking time to plan the vacation will help create a pleasurable and enjoyable vacation.

Air travel. Although the airline rules can change at anytime, the current rules as of this writing restrict the type of items you can carry on your flight.

Carry-on Rules
- 3 oz. or smaller containers for all liquids or gels
- Place those containers in **one** clear plastic quart-size zip lock bag

- Items must fit comfortably and can not be overstuffed in zip lock bag
- One zip lock bag per traveler
- Declare medication and baby items

For up-to-date air travel regulations, access www.tsa.gov. This is one rule you definitely want to know before you go.

Airlines could have different rules for bag size requirements for carry on and checked baggage. Be sure to consult with your airline for their specific rules before you travel.

Cruise travel. All cruise vacations offer excursions while at various ports. To save yourself time and maintain your budget, request a copy of the excursion brochure prior to your vacation. Take the time to study your options and choose the ones that are best for you. By planning ahead, you avoid having to make an impulsive decision right after boarding. It is also extremely important that you complete all paperwork for your cruise before you leave home.

Generally if you travel outside the country, you will need a passport. Passport information for U. S. Citizens can be found at www.travel.state.gov.

Automobile travel. Complete an overall pre-trip inspection of your vehicle. This includes checking spare tire, jack, and tire pressure. Also check oil and coolant levels. Don't forget to fill your windshield wiper fluid. Map out your route and itinerary. Book your hotel reservations ahead of time. Having something unexpected happen can dampen your vacation. Therefore, check your car for emergency travel kit items and restock if needed.

Emergency Travel Kit

Heavy Duty Backpack or Bag
Light Stick
Tow Rope
Jumper Cables
First Aid Kit
Fire Extinguisher
Blankets
Waterproof Poncho
Swiss Style Army Knife
Flashlight (the windup kind that doesn't require batteries)
Flat Tire Fixer
Drinking Water with 5 year shelf life
Leather Palm Work Gloves
Whistle with Lanyard
Emergency Instructions
Help Sign
Duct Tape, 10 yards
Utility Knife
Reflecting Triangle
Wet Nap Hand Cleaner

Packing. According to the Bureau of Transportation, 10,089 bags were lost, or delayed, daily in August 2006. If you are traveling on a vacation where someone else is responsible for the transportation of your luggage, you need to "cross-pack." If you are traveling with more than one bag, simply diversify your clothes among multiple bags. Split your toiletries and clothing categories among different suitcases. In other words, break the organizing golden rule of keeping like things together. In this case, mix all your items up so you have a good sampling of all items in each of your suitcases.

A few years ago, my husband and I took a cruise out of Miami, Florida, to the Bahamas. We had one large suitcase and one small suitcase. As we were boarding the ship, we handed our two suitcases to the appropriate staff and made our way onto the boat. The procedure in this situation is that the luggage gets loaded onto the vessel and the ship's staff delivers the suitcases to the appropriate stateroom. We had cruised several times before, so we expected to find our suitcases placed outside our stateroom door. The ship had left port and set sail. We headed to our room and found the small suitcase outside our door. We were pretty sure the other bag would arrive. However, time went by, and no suitcase. To make a long story short, our suitcase never arrived. We sailed the entire cruise without it, and returned home without it too.

I had done some cross-packing, but realized very quickly I had not done enough. My husband's suit for the formal night was in the suitcase that never arrived. Luckily ships have tuxedos available. The ship rented him a tuxedo and shoes free-of-charge, but they had no black dress socks and neither did my husband. This may have been a minor inconvenience, but the fact all my underwear for the week was in the lost suitcase was an issue.

While the Caribbean has some great shops for buying jewelry and liquor, lingerie is practically nowhere to be found. We had to get off the commercialized beaten path. The only underwear I could find to buy resembled the high briefs like our 5-year old daughter wore. And my husband was kind enough to point that out one romantic evening in our room.

The other major aggravation for my husband was that his contact lens supplies and eyeglasses were in the lost luggage. The infirmary was able to give him some sterile saline solution for inserting and storing his contacts. However, no contact case was anywhere to be found. So, I quickly informed our cabin steward not to dump the two glasses of water-looking substances down the sink! Additionally, there was no watching TV in bed for my husband after he took out his contacts…remember his eyeglasses were in the lost luggage. Actually, he could watch TV, he just couldn't see anything!

The other lesson learned from this experience is that I also inventory the items I pack in my luggage whenever cruising or flying. It is much easier to submit an insurance claim when having a reliable complete inventory list on hand than to recreate one after the luggage is gone. We spent several hours one evening of our cruise completing insurance claim paperwork. It wasn't something I imagined doing on my vacation!

I know you might be wondering. Did we ever get our lost luggage back? Five days after we returned from our cruise, and eleven days after we handed our bag to the cruise staff, the lost piece of luggage showed up on our doorstep at home. The bit of good news...all the items were, of course, still clean. No dirty laundry for me.

Will I cruise again? Absolutely, but I will definitely do a better job cross-packing!

The moral of traveling and vacations: Whether traveling for holiday or business, take the time to plan appropriately. Remember, patience and attitude is often the difference between a good experience and a bad one.

TOLL FREE NUMBERS
Airlines

Aeromexico	www.aeromexico.com	800-237-6639
Air Canada	www.aircanada.com	888-247-2262
Air France	www.airfrance.com	800-237-2747
Air Jamaica	www.airjamaica.com	800-523-5585
Air New Zealand	www.airnewzealand.com	800-262-1234
Alaska Airlines	www.alaskaair.com	800-426-0333
Alitalia	www.alitalia.com	800-223-5730
American Airlines	www.aa.com	800-433-7300
Bahamasair	www.bahamasair.com	800-222-4262
British Airways	www.britishairways.com	800-247-9297
CanJet Airlines	www.canjet.com	800-809-7777
China Airlines	www.china-airlines.com	800-227-5118
Continental Airlines	www.continental.com	800-523-3273
Delta Air Lines	www.delta.com	800-221-1212
EgyptAir	www.egyptair.com	800-334-6787
Frontier Airlines	www.frontierairlines.com	800-432-1359
Hawaiian Airlines	www.hawaiianair.com	800-367-5320
Horizon Air	horizonair.alaskaair.com	800-547-9308
Japan Airlines	www.jal.com	800-525-3663
JetBlue Airways	www.jetblue.com	800-538-2583
Korean Air	www.koreanair.com	800-438-5000
Lufthansa	portal.lufthansa.com	800-399-5838
Mexicana	www.mexicana.com	800-531-7921
Northwest/KLM Airlines	www.nwa.com	800-225-2525
Olympic Airlines	www.olympicairlines.com	800-223-1226
Pan Am	www.flypanam.com	800-359-7262
Qantas Airways	www.qantas.com	800-227-4500
Southwest Airlines	www.southwest.com	800-435-9792
SWISS	www.swiss.com	877-359-7947
Thai Airways	www.thaiairways.com	800-426-5204

| United Airlines | www.united.com | 800-864-8331 |
| US Airways | www.usairways.com | 800-428-4322 |

Automobile Rentals

Alamo Rent-A-Car	www.alamo.com	877-222-9075
Avis Rent-A-Car	www.avis.com	800-230-4898
Budget Rent-A-Car	www.budget.com	800-527-0700
Courtesy Auto Rental	www.courtesyauto.com	800-222-6741
Discount Car	www.discountcar.com	800-263-2355
Dollar Rent-A-Car	www.dollar.com	800-800-3665
Enterprise Rent-A-Car	www.enterprise.com	800-261-7331
Hertz Rent-A-Car	www.hertz.com	800-654-3131
National Car Rental	www.nationalcar.com	877-222-9058
Payless Car Rental	www.paylesscarrental.com	800-729-5377
Rent-A-Wreck	www.rentawreck.com	877-877-0700
Thrifty Car Rental	www.thrifty.com	800-367-2277
U-Save Auto Rental of America Inc.	www.usave.net	800-438-2300

Hotels & Motels

Adam's Mark Hotels & Resorts	www.adamsmark.com	800-444-2326
Baymont Inns & Suites	www.baymontinns.com	877-229-6668
Best Western	www.bestwestern.com	800-780-7234
Choice Hotels	www.choicehotels.com	877-424-6423
Comfort Inns	www.comfortinn.com	877-424-6423
Days Inns	www.daysinn.com	800-329-7466

Doubletree Hotels	www.doubletree.com	800-222-8733
Econo Lodges	www.econolodge.com	877-424-6423
Embassy Suites	www.embassysuites.com	800-362-2779
Four Seasons Hotels & Resorts	www.fourseasons.com	800-819-5053
Hampton Inns	www.hamptoninn.com	800-426-7866
Hilton Hotels	www.hilton.com	800-445-8667
Holiday Inn	www.holiday-inn.com	888-465-4329
Howard Johnson	www.hojo.com	800-446-4656
Hyatt Hotels & Resorts	www.hyatt.com	888-591-1234
Inns of America	www.innsofamerica.com	800-826-0778
Knights Inn	www.knightsinn.com	800-843-5644
La Quinta Inns	www.lq.com	800-753-3757
Marriott Hotels, Resorts & Suites	www.marriott.com	888-236-2427
Motel 6	www.motel6.com	800-466-8356
Omni Hotels	www.omnihotels.com	888-444-6664
Quality Inns	www.qualityinn.com	877-424-6423
Radisson Hotels	www.radisson.com	800-395-7046
Ramada	www.ramada.com	800-272-6232
Red Carpet Inns	www.bookroomsnow.com	800-251-1962
Red Lion Hotels and Inns	www.redlion.com	800-733-5466
Red Roof Inns	www.redroof.com	800-733-7663
Resort Quest International	www.resortquest.com	800-467-3529
Sheraton Hotels	www.sheraton.com	800-325-3535
Super 8	www.super8.com	800-800-8000
Travelodge	www.travelodge.com	800-578-7878
Westin Hotels & Resorts	www.westin.com	800-937-8461
Wyndham Hotels & Resorts	www.wyndham.com	877-999-3223

International Working Cell Phones

Cellhire USA	www.cellhire.com	888-476-7368
Inc Worldcell	www.worldcell.com	888-967-5323
InTouch USA	www.intouchusa.com	800-872-7626
RoadPost	www.roadpost.com	888-290-1616
Cellular Abroad	www.cellularabroad.com	800-287-5072
Mind Logic	www.mindlogic.com	877-327-5076

QUICK TIP: When traveling, stuff socks and other small items into shoes to maximize space and offer support to your shoes.

Katherine Lawerence, Space Matters
Richmond, Virginia

Chapter 19

ORGANIZING YOUR KIDS

"Rules are essential in order for any family to operate smoothly."

-Scott Heaton, LMFT & Traci Heaton, <u>Accountable Kids</u>

How many times have we asked our children, "why do you keep leaving your things on the table?" Or, the kitchen counter? Or, the coffee table? Or, the dining room table? "Please put your things away!"

Where can they temporarily store their possessions? Always expecting them to keep all of their daily items in their rooms may not be the answer.

Where do you keep <u>your</u> daily papers and projects? Most of us have designated temporary space for our things in the main living areas of our homes. We put things in files, bins, baskets, or on desktops. Then we periodically go through them, completing paperwork, transferring to permanent filing areas, walking items to their homes, and purging.

Create space in the main living area for your kids, too! It could be bins, or baskets, in the mudroom - or even right in the kitchen. This "temporary home" for items creates advantages for all household members. The kids (and spouse) know where to find the things they are looking for, and they also know where to put other family member's items during a quick cleanup. This can create a sense of ownership and responsibility for each person's possessions.

Since organization is a learned skill, kids also must be taught how to maintain this space. Periodically go through the items with them and help them make decisions on what to do with each thing. Papers can periodically be purged. Toys should be put in their designated areas – kid's rooms/playrooms/toy boxes. If this is a new toy, talk about where its home should be. Each item should ultimately have a home.

Be careful of that elusive home for personal possessions called "away." We ask our children to put things "away" without considering the possibility that they do no know where "away" is! This is why it is important to practice the process with them. Involve them in the process now, and as adults, they will be way ahead of the game!

> **QUICK TIP:** *When traveling with young children pack each daily outfit in a store brand gallon size zipper bags you can easily fit a diaper, washcloth, socks, shirt and pants. It will save you time getting dressed at a relatives' home or hotel. You can also pack extra diapers, wipes, etc. in zipper bags. This also saves room in your suitcase because you can squeeze all the air out and create flat "packages" for packing (not to mention saving spills or messy baggage checks). On the way home, the bags can be used for dirty clothes, local purchases or liquids in the diaper bag/carry on. Back home you can use the bags for a final time on dog walks.*
>
> **Carolyn Anderson Fermann,**
> **Simply Organized Life**
> **Dexter, Michigan**

Chapter 20

BACK TO SCHOOL TIME

'Keep back-to-school time from becoming berserk by getting things in order before the first day."

-Scholastic.com

The familiar feelings surface every August. There is excitement, nervousness, and apprehension as children head back to school. Are your children ready for school when August rolls around? With the appropriate planning, you can find the transition back to school a breeze.

Bedtime Routine
Set a bedtime routine you adhere to every evening. Be sure to include organizing the backpack, laying out clothes for the next day, and packing lunch if needed. Making a list of tasks to be completed in the morning will create more time, and reduce stress, in the morning. Set the table for breakfast before heading to bed.

Morning Routine
Like the bedtime routine, it is critical that a morning routine be created and followed daily. Reviewing your task list, created the night before, should be a component of every morning. Set aside enough time to double check that backpacks and lunches are ready to go. Limit TV viewing to a minimum, if at all. If the TV is viewed in the morning use it as a reward, if - and only if - the child is completely ready to walk out the door.

Homework
Encourage your child to complete their homework as soon as they get home from school. Of course, allow 15 minutes or so initially to unpack their backpack and re-fuel with a snack before hitting the books. Getting into this habit eliminates the propensity to procrastinate and teaches them the skill and importance of planning and time management.

Juggling Extra-Curricular Activities
A family calendar is a must for every active family. Consider using a different color ink or highlighter for each different family member's activities. Additionally, it is imperative the calendar be accessible to all family members. If mom and dad share their time at activities, note on the calendar if it will be mom or dad that will be taking or picking up the child for the activity. Take care not to over-schedule your child and be sure to allow time for

traveling, dinner, and downtime. Make good use of your time in the car. It's a great time for your child to read, or practice his or her spelling.

A routine is something that is done over and over again the same way. Kids function best in situations where they know what to expect. Routines do just that!

Additionally, keep in mind planning is the most important key to an enjoyable school year and childhood. Take advantage of this opportunity to set in place some positive life-long habits.

QUICK TIP: Make extra breakfast food and freeze it for a busy morning. Extra pancakes, muffins, breakfast casserole, etc can really be a lifesaver when you are short on time!

Joetta Tucker, My Organizing Friend
Geneva, New York

Chapter 21

TANGLED IN THE TINSEL
●●●

If you celebrate annual holidays, in November and December you probably find yourself overwhelmed at some point. Ironically, that is just the opposite of what you should be feeling. The good news is there are some specific steps you can take to get a handle on the chaos and enjoy the true meaning of these holidays.

6 Holiday Organizing Ideas

Bah Humbug!

Do you sometimes feel like "scrooge" when it comes to the thought of the holidays? Is getting ready for the holidays overwhelming? Here are a few simple ideas to help you get organized.

1. HOLIDAY DECLUTTERING. November and December are the perfect times to clean out the kitchen closets and cupboards. This will lend itself to an organized kitchen for meal preparation and baking. This is also an ideal time to file away those stacks of papers. If the papers don't have a home, create one. Set up a paper management system. Hire a professional organizer if needed.

2. SORTING & WEEDING. Clean out the old to make room for the new! Get rid of toys that your children have outgrown, are broken, or are no longer of interest to them. The same goes for the clothing closets. If you haven't worn it in the last year, sell it or donate it. Take advantage of the end of the year tax write-offs.

3. GATHERING GIFT IDEAS. Once you come across an idea, place the idea in a folder titled "gift ideas." It is a great place for saving those catalogs or sale ads with ideas. If the item is in a catalog, circle the item. You can tear out the page, and the ordering information, staple them together and write the name of the person who corresponds with this gift idea. Or, if you choose to keep the catalog intact, write the page number on the front of the catalog for easy reference. When returning to the catalog, this notation will "tell" you the only reason you saved this catalog is for the pages identified on the front. Hence no need to duplicate your time perusing the entire catalog again!

4. TRACKING GIFTS PURCHASED. Set up a system for tracking the gifts you have bought. This system will avoid costly duplication and over-buying. You can keep this information in a notebook, on your computer, or you can use the form included in the Home Operations Made Easy Organizer. You can find information on this product on page 206.

5. BAKING FOR THE HOLIDAYS. Make a list of the items you wish to bake. Gather your recipes and determine what ingredients you need to buy. If you plan to do a great deal of baking, consider baking ahead of time and freezing. If you don't want to freeze the items, mix up the dry ingredients in a zip lock bag and label it appropriately. It will be ready to mix with the wet ingredients and bake. Schedule your baking time on your calendar. Using your calendar allows you to space out your baking and confirm there is enough time to get it all done before the holidays arrive!

6. DECORATION STORAGE. After the holidays, it is important to return your decorations to "organized storage." This will make next year's decorating simple and carefree. Store your decorations in appropriately labeled containers. Sort, organize, and store by groupings of like items.

How to FINALLY Get Organized for the New Year

Put Away the Holiday Décor: Make sure you have put away your décor as outlined in the 6 Steps to Holiday Organizing above.

Gather and Organize the Holiday Photos: Get your photos developed and/or printed. Many stores have opportunities where you can send your digital photos over the Internet and pick up the printed photos at the store at your leisure. Or you can use the simple self-serve kiosks located in all the major big-box stores.

If you scrapbook, now is the time to complete this task while the holidays are still fresh in your mind. Otherwise, slip the photos into albums or photo boxes right now rather than letting this job build up and create a mountain of clutter. Take care to use photo safe albums and supplies.

Make Notes from the Holiday Events: Jot down notes about what worked and what did not work for this holiday season. Write down suggestions for next year. For example, if you discovered during this year's holiday meal that it was the last time the "kids" should eat at the big table, make a note to move the "kids" to their own dinner table next year. Or, if Aunt Emily was allergic to the corn casserole dish, you will want to make a note to offer an alternate corn dish next year. File these notes in a place you will be able to find them next year.

Go Through Your Financial Records from Last Year: Dispose of the records no longer needed while cleaning out your system to make room for the financial records from the New Year. Be sure to keep those records needed to support your tax returns. If you don't have a system in place for retaining those monthly financial records, now is a great time to set up that system. Creating a home and system for these records is a wonderful resolution for the New Year. Refer to Chapter 7 for specifics on organizing your tax records.

Set Up New Systems of Organization: A system of organization can be created for any area, or item in the household or office. Creating and placing an item in its home eliminates clutter and creates organization. When setting up systems of retaining paperwork, keep in mind that 80% of the papers you file away are never referenced or looked at again! Be selective in the materials you choose to retain!

Gather Items Needed for Tax Returns: April will be here before you know it! Start gathering items needed for completing your tax return. As you receive those "Important Retain for Tax Purposes" items in the mail, be sure to place them all together in one place. If you don't already have a system in place for maintaining these records throughout the year, now is the time to set up that system. Label a file folder or manila envelope "Tax Info for 20XX." As you receive items throughout the year, simply place them in this envelope or folder. When tax time rolls around, you will have those documents you need to complete your tax return! Take your organization one step further and set up folders as outlined in Chapter 7.

Resolve to "Get Organized!" this Year: Make a list of 12 areas or rooms that you wish to get organized. Commit to tackling these areas--one per month. Believe it or not, many people find organizing refreshes and invigorates them. As you organize you will feel the weight of chaos and clutter lifted from your shoulders…it truly is a New Year!

Face it, getting organized is probably one of your top new year's resolutions. Make this the year you FINALLY do it!

QUICK TIP: Do you have space in your cabinets to hold the holiday dishes? If not - simply rotate them for the season. Store your regular dishes whenever you bring out the holiday dishes. Holiday recipes along with your holiday dishes can be kept in storage until next year.

Joetta Tucker, My Organizing Friend
Geneva, New York

Chapter 22

DON'T SHOP 'TILL YOU DROP!

●●●

Shopping and errands can be time-consuming endeavors. Have you ever found yourself spending the entire day running from one errand to another and not really accomplishing much? This is stressful to say the least. With gas prices, it is down right expensive too.

Planning is the key to making the most out of shopping and errands. Before you leave the house, make a list of all the places you need to go. Also have a list of each item you need to get or task you need to complete for each stop you make. Evaluate all your stops, then start with the errand farthest from home, and work your way back home. As you make the stops, check them off your list.

Shopping lists are critical to stress-free, efficient, and cost-effective shopping. If you have a list of all the items you need, stick to the list and it will save you money. You will also be in and out of the store and on your way to your next destination in no time at all.

Keep a running shopping list at home. A shopping list on the refrigerator, on or in a cabinet door, or any other sensible location in the kitchen is a major time and money-saver. Anytime you or a family member notices something running out, add it to the list. Take the list with you to the store, and check off the items as you place them in the cart.

Avoid shopping during the busiest shopping times. Saturdays and early evening are generally busy times, as is Christmas Eve. Consider shopping late at night or early in the morning, as there are less people and more parking spaces.

Once arriving home from shopping and errands, you should promptly put all items away. If you have cold items, put these away into the refrigerator and freezer first. Then empty each and every bag putting the items away in their designated homes. If an item is new to the household, designate a home immediately and put it away. If you have gifts for the holiday, consider wrapping them right away. Leaving your purchases in their bags is simply creating clutter.

Remember, the telephone is a valuable tool. If you question whether or not a store might have what you need, or where the item you want is located, call ahead! If possible, request the store hold the item at the front counter. A few minutes on the telephone can save an hour or more of your time.

Instituting a well-planned day will reduce your stress, and leave time for you to enjoy the things that really matter in life. Enjoy the shopping, just don't do the dropping!

QUICK TIP: Plan all dinners for the week, with your family if possible. Write your grocery list from the menus, fill in other needed items then go grocery shopping ONCE a week! If it's not on the list, it doesn't get purchased until the next week.

Donna Olsen, From Chaos to Calm
Brockport, New York

Chapter 23

YOU CAN'T TAKE IT WITH YOU
●●●

We live in a society of excess and are constantly bombarded with marketing and impulse buying. It is not unusual for our stuff to become an extension of who we are. Unfortunately, when this happens we lose sight of what is really important.

I spent some time a while ago helping clean out the home of a dear friend of mine who died from a massive stroke. Neither the family, nor his friends, really knew what to do with the stuff that had belonged to him. As we sifted through his belongings what was really important became clear. None of the clothes, linens, furniture, or even the food left in the refrigerator, was important. It is life that is important, not the stuff.

Although Jim had been a friend of mine for many years, I never had the opportunity to visit his home until after his passing. I was very pleased to see Jim lived a simple life. He did not wrap himself up in all kinds of stuff. He had a limited number of possessions, and because of that, possessions did not steal his time and energy. He actually had time to enjoy things in life.

Take a moment and look around your home. Are you surrounded with only those things that add value to your life? If not, it's time to make some room to enjoy life.

First, declare your home at maximum capacity - and stop bringing stuff in. Next, start with a room, a cupboard or a box. Go through each item one-by-one. Keep only those things that add value to your life. Everything else goes away.

Just like what was discussed in chapter 15, this process is called S-WEE-P™ (Sort, WEEd, Purge). Your sorting categories might be: family, friends, donation, consignment, trash, recycle and, lastly, keep. Be ruthless. Your life enjoyment depends on it.

Depending on your accumulation of stuff, it could take weeks, months, or even years to let go of the excess. Nevertheless, keep plugging away. With each box, cupboard, and room you clear out, you are that much closer to having time to enjoy life. Since you can't take it with you, you might as well stop it from stealing your life.

Now go make some room to enjoy life!

QUICK TIP: Think of your home as a business. Your items (clutter) are the employees. Interview each item. If one is not "working" for you, or does not have a place within your home daily, weekly, monthly, or yearly. FIRE IT! ... now get it out of your home.

Deborah Erickson, No Where But Up, Organizing
Hemlock, Michigan

Chapter 24

THINK MULTI-USE
●●●

Take note: The newest item on the market is not always better. Mistakenly, many people are lulled into a false belief that a new gadget must be better than the one they already have. If you follow this thought process, you will likely end up with two, or more, items that do the same thing. Case in point is the revolving pizza oven.

While it is a very cool gadget, it also requires some serious storage space. As a professional organizer, I would ask you, "Can't you use your regular oven to bake a pizza?"

Last week I challenged a client to "think multi-use." Her process for duplication was not adding a new updated version to the mix, but rather having multiples of the same type of item designated for different but similar uses.

Let me explain. She had twelve leaf rakes, only two people in her family, and she was adamant she was going to keep all twelve rakes.

When I questioned whether she used all of them, I received a surprising response. Yes, she did use all of them regularly. With a puzzled look on my face, I asked her to explain under what circumstances she used the different rakes. She shared with me if there are only a few leaves, she uses the smaller rake. If there are more leaves, she uses the bigger rake. Sometimes, she likes to use the longer handle rake so she does not need to bend down so much. But the shorter handle comes in handy if she is on the hill. To make a long story short, she had a scenario for using each of her twelve rakes.

When she was all done, I asked her "What would happen if you had only two small rakes, plus the two bigger rakes, and let go of the other eight rakes?" While she knew the answer, she was not ready to verbalize it, and that was okay. However, I did ask her to consider multi-use.

On the other hand, if you often find yourself buying the newest upgraded gadget, it probably means you are either looking for the easy answer, or the rush of buying it propels a feeling of self-esteem. Either way, you are probably looking in the wrong place.

Instead, look at what you already own and ask yourself, "Can I make do with what I have, and is what I already own capable of reaching the same result?" If the answer is yes, bypass the new gadget, and rediscover the items you already own.

Now go sort through your items and think multi-use!

QUICK TIP: Maximize your kitchen storage space by having multifunctional utensils. Donate single purpose items that take up valuable space and rarely get used.

Stephanie Manawil, Organized in Style
Orange County, California

Chapter 25

Holy Cow:
What God Says About Clutter
●●●

*"Take Care! Be on your guard against all kinds
of Greed: for one's life does not consist in the
abundance of possessions."*
                                -Luke 12:15

So, do you hear what God is saying in this
reading? Not only is it okay to let go of your stuff,
He is encouraging it. God does not want you to be
bound by your possessions.

Do you find your stuff controlling your life?
Everything you own is a thief of your time and
energy. God has other plans for you. He does not
want you stressed and anxious over the clutter, and
stuff, in your life.

In the book of Matthew, Chapter 6, Verses 19-20, teachings about money and possessions are shared.

"Don't store up treasures here on earth, where moths eat them and rust destroys them, and where thieves break in and steal. Store your treasures in heaven, where moths and rust cannot destroy, and thieves do not break in and steal."

As a professional organizer I have seen my share of moth eaten and rust destroyed items. I have also worked with a client who had thieves break in and steal paperwork. This resulted in her identity being stolen.

Logically, the more unnecessary paperwork you have in your home containing personal identification, the more information a thief has to steal. Plus, the more paperwork you have, the easier it is to find.

Verse 24 goes onto say, "No one can serve two masters. For you will hate one and love the other; you will be devoted to one and despise the other. You cannot serve both God and money."

In this teaching, money represents your clutter, your stuff. God is saying that you cannot focus all your energy on your stuff and serve God at the same time.

If your life is controlled and driven by boxes, piles, and mounds of stuff, God wants you to let go and find the peace He has waiting for you.

I encourage you to prayerfully consider your relationship with your stuff. Is it keeping you from serving God? Is it causing you anxiety or stress? If so, do something about it! Hire a professional organizer, seek out a therapist or consult a psychologist. It is "okay" to ask for help. That's why God has surrounded you with opportunities for support.

Do not put this off! The scripture of Luke 14:16-24 is a Parable of the Great Feast. Grab your Bible and read through it. You will find God's story to reflect that those who procrastinate lose out.

QUICK TIP: *Try de-cluttering your linen closet. Check with local animal shelters to see if they have a need for your old towels, blankets and sheets. A local shelter can be found at www.pets911.com. They may also appreciate cleaning products that you've kept, but don't use*

Joetta Tucker, My Organizing Friend
Geneva, New York

Chapter 26

ORGANIZE YOUR FINANCIAL HEALTH

●●●

If the stock market is down, job security is worrisome, and paying bills is a struggle, your financial health may need some improving. In this type of economic climate, organizing your finances is beyond critical.

One of the most vital components of organizing is planning. When it comes to financial health, creating a budget is your best form of planning. A budget is a goal or guiding point. Its initial purpose is to find out where your money goes. It is only once you know where your money goes that you can make some informed changes to improve your financial health.

To create a budget, you need the following:
1) **Income.** Gather all your pay stubs and other documentation of income. If you have automatic deposits, you may need to reference your banking statements.
2) **Fixed Expenses.** These are expenses that you have every month, quarter, or year. Examples of these are mortgage, car loans, utilities, insurance, tuition etc.
3) **Variable Expenses.** These are expenses that vary by category. Some months you may have them and some months you may not. The amounts likely vary each month, too. Example of these may be clothing, medical bills, repairs, travel, gifts, donations, entertainment, etc.

After you have gathered documentation of each of the above, plug the categories into your budget or use a budget template. There is a great free template for household budgets available at http://www.vertex42.com/ExcelTemplates/monthly-household-budget.html

For your budget, the numbers you plug into the categories represent an ideal or financial goal. Once you have your budget in place, you will now need to track the actual amount of money spent for a given month. With the free template identified above, plug the actual numbers in the appropriate column.

By readily comparing your budget to your actual spending you can make changes as appropriate and improve your fiscal health. Maintaining your actual spending isn't difficult, it just takes a bit of discipline and persistence. With this bit of organizing and forethought you can contour your finances and ultimately sharpen your financial health.

QUICK TIP: Where is your critical information? If a disaster occurred, could you pick it up and leave without having to hunt for it? If not, how can you correct that?

Teresa Spruill
Spruill Money Management and Organization Services
Smithsburg, Maryland

Chapter 27

GET A GRIP ON SPENDING
●●●

In the last chapter we covered budgeting. In this chapter we are taking it one step further. We are outlining how to organize your spending. With the status of the economy, you might be concerned about your finances and keeping more money in your pocket than ever before.

I have good news for you. There are four specific actions you can implement to get you going in the right direction.

1) **Track your automatic teller machine (ATM) withdrawals.** While this might take discipline on your part to do this, it can keep you from being overdrawn and save you a headache in the long run. If you fail to track

your withdrawals, you will not have a true picture of your financial situation.

2) **Use a shopping list and stick to it.** Keep a running list in your kitchen. Add items to it as they are depleted. When it is time to go shopping, buy only those items on your list. You can save yourself oodles of money if you stay away from the impulsive items at the store. Also, never go to the grocery store on an empty stomach as you will spend way more money and likely end up with lots of junk food!

3) **Use just one credit card.** Paying with cash is by far the best way to manage your money, but if you must use a credit card, only use one. I have seen way too many clients late on paying their credit card bills, often because they lost them, or overlooked paying them. The more credit cards you actively use, the more bills you will need to pay and the more work for you to do. Furthermore, to keep a handle on your finances pay your monthly credit card bills on time and in full.

4) **Sleep on it.** If you come across something at a store you think you want, and it is not a necessity, put it back on the shelf. Go home and sleep on it. Then, after 24 hours, if you still want the item, go back to the store and get it. Chances are you won't want it badly enough the next day to make a special trip to buy it.

If you put these four simple systems into place, you will be successful in keeping more money in your pocket.

Now go get a grip on your spending!

QUICK TIP: *To help remember birthdays and other important reoccurring events, buy a small hanging calendar (about 7" x 14" when open) & hang on your refrigerator for each month put a 3" x 3" Post-it note and list the birthdays, anniversaries & repeat for each month. If someone's birthday is the first of the month, put them on the previous month's note. Then you can send a card in time. When the month is over, store the Post-It note on the last page of the calendar for re-use next year.*

Cathy Bock, Chaos Tamers LLC
Northbrook, Illinois

Chapter 28

THINK OUTSIDE THE BOX
●●●

People often get stuck in one manner of thinking. If it isn't in their tunnel of vision, it does not exist as an option. This type of thinking limits you and your opportunities.

Habits are significantly difficult to break away from. Your thoughts and thinking patterns are no different. If your habit of mentally processing something is in one manner, it is difficult to think differently. By learning how to "think outside the box'" of your normal thinking pattern, you will discover opportunities to grow and improve your efficiency, as well as the productivity of your processes.

Here are two key questions that will stretch your mind to "think outside the box":

1) Is there only one way to reach my desired outcome? Generally, this answer is no.
2) What is another way I can reach my desired outcome? If you can't figure it out on your own, solicit help from a friend, neighbor, or a professional organizer.

A few years back, I heard from someone who had jumped outside the box. The day after I presented an organizing seminar, I received an email from one of the participants.

Her email explained: Before the seminar, she and her husband were certain their laundry room was too small. In fact, they had obtained designs and plans to knock down walls, rework the plumbing and expand the laundry room. It was a major, and expensive, remodeling project.

From the seminar, the participant recognized she was stuck inside a box. Her inherent thinking was a laundry room needed plenty of room to store all the dirty clothes in the household. She was stuck on this thinking, so her mind was focused on discovering "how to make the room big enough to contain all the dirty clothes."

At some point during the seminar she realized her real goal was to eliminate and control the overwhelming dirty clothes in the laundry room. She came to the realization that increasing the size of the room wasn't the only option.

Something in the seminar sparked her thinking. Instead of having overflowing dirty laundry in the laundry room, she was simply going to buy laundry baskets for each of the bedrooms. Voila! No piles of dirty clothes in the laundry room and thousands of dollars saved on the remodel. She had jumped outside the box.
You can too.

Stand up, open the lid, and jump out of the box. You are on your way to more options for an organized life!

QUICK TIP: *Are you hanging onto manuals for every item you've EVER owned? Well - recycle them and free up space! If you need one, you can download just about any owner's manual for free at www.safemanuals.com.*

Joetta Tucker, My Organizing Friend
Geneva,New York

Chapter 29

SET SMART ORGANIZING GOALS

"Each of us needs to see and sense what is significant in order to clarify our vision of success."

-Judy Siebert, *Exploring Productivity*

Setting goals is an integral component to accomplishing your desired outcomes. However, there is an art to setting goals. If you have set unrealistic goals, you have likely set yourself up for failure. By setting **SMART** goals, you have a greater chance at reaching them.

First of all, choose the area or project you want to get organized. Once you have that in mind, apply the **SMART** technique. Just remember **SMART**; it is the acronym to reaching your goals.

S-pecific. Your goal must be as specific as possible. Is it clear, distinct, and explicit? It must be well defined.

M-easurable. The goal must be measurable. You must be able to measure your progress. How will you know if you accomplish it?

A-chievable. Your goal must be achievable, or attainable. Do you have everything you need, or can you get what you need, in order to achieve your goal? Do you know the steps needed to execute? Are you willing to do those steps?

R-ealistic. The goal must be realistic. Is your goal practical and reasonable? Lower your expectations if need be.

T-imely. You must define a due-date. Without a deadline, the likelihood of reaching your goal is almost nil.

To pull it all together, here is an example of a **SMART** organizing goal: "I will clear off the accumulation of papers on the dining room table by Easter weekend."

This is a **SMART** goal. **Specific=** clearing papers; **Measurable=** I will know I have reached my goal when I have a clear table; **Achievable=** I know where most of the papers go; **Realistic=** I have two months to do it, it can be done; **Timely=** it needs to be done by Easter weekend.

For good measure, here is a non-**SMART** goal: "I will organize the entire house by next week." Unless you live in an efficiency apartment with no stuff this isn't a **SMART** goal. While it may be specific, measurable, and timely - it likely can't be achieved, nor is it realistic.

Goals are easier to set than to accomplish, but if you are **SMART** about it, you can do it!

Now, go get **SMART** and set your goals to get organized!

QUICK TIP: Dedicate just 15 minutes per day to straightening up, and the clutter won't reach overwhelming proportions!

Lauren Silverman, Moreganized
Skokie, Illinois

Chapter 30

GET YOURSELF A NAG BUDDY

*"Probably the main reason we put things off
is we are not organized to do a job."*

-Sandra Felton, <u>The New Messies Manual</u>

It is no secret. You know that planning and preparing is the first route to getting things done. Unfortunately, that is not enough. You also need to implement.

Failing to do so often comes down to the awful human nature of procrastinating.

Why do you put things off? Why is procrastination so easy? How can you combat the procrastination tendencies?

Often times, you put off doing things because they are too difficult or because you are not sure how to do something. Other times, items may be put on the back burner because something more fun, or easier to do, comes along. Moreover, you may convince yourself that you don't really need to do that because "what's the likelihood of needing it."

There are five (5) steps you can take to minimize procrastination.

1) **Set a hard deadline.** Without a deadline it is way too convenient and easy to shuffle things to the bottom of the pile.

2) **Find a nag buddy, or motivational partner, and share your deadline with them.** Now, you are accountable to someone else and this will greatly increase the likelihood of completing the project or task.

3) **Give yourself rewards.** As you progress forward with your task or project, pat yourself on your back with rewards along the way.

4) **Break the project or task into small workable pieces.** Consider working on the project for a set amount of time rather than a set amount of work.

5) **Work on the project when you are at your best.** If you are a morning person, attack the project

in the morning. Likewise, if you are a night owl, work on it at night.

Unfortunately, there is no magic wand to wave over the stuff you don't want to do. However, with some sound strategies, strong self-discipline, and help from a buddy, you can accomplish the things you want and need to do.

QUICK TIP: I know my personality type very well, and I require a little pressure to meet my deadlines. So when I'm tempted to procrastinate, I look for ways to turn the task or project into a game and find ways to make it FUN! It may be as simple as putting the paperwork in a bright colored file folder and printing out a fun piece of clipart and taping it to the front. Or it may mean breaking the project into smaller chunks and celebrating the completion of each chunk with a small incentive of some sort. Focusing on the RELIEF of finally getting the project completed, though, is sometimes the BEST incentive of all.

Julie Perrine, CPS/CAP
All Things Admin
Hiawatha, Iowa

Chapter 31

TO-DO LIST MASTER

"The effective use of lists is critical to any well-organized time management system."

-Stephanie Winston, <u>Getting Organized</u>

Do you have days that you never seem to get anything accomplished? Many times this happens as a result of poor planning. Establishing systems is a key component to organization. A system for planning your "to-do" items is critical. No doubt there are numerous systems for maintaining and utilizing to-do lists. Different systems work for different people.

I generally recommend utilizing a two-list system. This system comes in handy especially on those days you are bombarded with things from all angles!

Two List System: 1) Master List; 2) Daily To-Do List.

For the Master List, I suggest a spiral notebook, or steno notebook. Something that is bound together and doesn't separate easily will do perfect. It is critical the pages stay together. If you prefer an electronic format, create a "Master List" folder on your computer, or handheld device. The purpose of the Master List is two-fold. One, it will eliminate all the sticky notes and scratch paper that get lost and misplaced. And two, it will allow you to have a place to store all those thoughts you have swimming in your head.

On the Master List, list each and every item or task that you have to do. Do not worry about priority, just write it down. Your Master List will be your safety net to make sure things do not fall through the cracks. You could have 20-30 tasks, or more, on your initial Master List.

You must know the whereabouts of your Master List at all times. It must be accessible so you can add to it each and every time you think of something that needs to be done.

Review your Master List daily, and make your daily To-Do List for the next day. I recommend this be accomplished at the end of each day, as it allows you to enjoy your evening more, and gives you a clear game plan for the next morning. Peruse your Master List and come up with 6-10 manageable items to do the next day. As you complete an item on your Daily To-Do List, be sure to cross it off the list. At the end of the day, carry any un-done tasks to the next day's Daily To-Do List. Review your Master List once again, taking care to cross off the items completed and copy items for the next day to your Daily To-Do list. Repeat this process daily. After 21 times or so, it will become habit.

If you have tried this system and it did not quite work for you, there is another less common system you may want to consider.

The "ABCDE System."

1)   Make your list of items to do.
2) Place an "A" next to the items that are absolutely critical. In other words, if you didn't get these done, you would be in big trouble or it would cost you or your company lots of money. (If you have multiple "A's", identify the tasks as "A-1," "A-2" and so on.)
3) Place a "B" next to the items that are important, but not nearly as critical as the "A" items.
4)   Place a "C" next to the items that don't have serious consequences if not completed. Obviously, these are less critical than the "B" items.
5) Place a "D" next to each of the items that can be delegated. Delegate anything someone else can do.

To be the most productive, you should only be doing the things that only you can do.

6)   Place an "E" next to every item you can eliminate.   It is common to over-extend, over-commit, and set unrealistic tasks for yourself. Only task those items that really make a difference in your job or life. Stop wasting your time on items that are of little or no value.

Rules of the "ABCDE System"

1)   You must do all "A" tasks first.
2)   You cannot do a "B" task if you have any outstanding "A" tasks on your list.
3)   Likewise, you can't do a "C" task before a "B" task.
4)   You must delegate those tasks that can be delegated. If you are not sure "how" to delegate, check out these websites.

     http://getmoredone.com/2010/08/how-to-delegate/

     http://www.zeromillion.com/business/management/delegating-work.html

5)   Get real and eliminate those items that don't have long-term consequences. Ask yourself, "In the grand scheme of things, does this really matter?"

Now, go create your "to-do list".

QUICK TIP: Create a master list in excel. A master list is a master list of everything you have to do. You may want to sort personal vs. business or create two separate lists. It could also be sorted by season or categories.

Eileen Roth, Everything in Its Place, Scottsdale, Arizona

Chapter 32

MANAGING THE DEMANDS OF YOUR JOB

●●●

"More than 90% [of people] declare an overwhelming sense of time-poverty, part of an epidemic of anxiety and pressure in our society."

- Psychology Today

It all starts with recognizing the demands you face every day. There are physical, mental, and time demands.

Physical demands: You are working longer hours. Much of this can be attributed to the fact you can be connected to your job 24/7. You have access to email no matter where you are located, whether logging in remotely from home, or from your cellular telephone. There is also physically more paper in today's society than there ever has been.

You have more paper to deal with so it is critical you have a system set up to manage that paper.

More technology requires you keep up with the latest software and new programs. These are all things you must keep up with or you will fall behind in the business world.

Mental demands: The volume of data has exponentially increased over the past ten years. You have more data and paper coming at you than ever before. You must have systems set in place to deal with all this, or you will find yourself mentally drained. Additionally, the speed of the changing technology and the constant learning of new technology is a mental burden.

Time demands: Because the world was going to go paperless, and technology was supposed to make things quicker and cut out work for everyone, you are expected to do more with less. Moreover, the status of the economy adds additional emphasis to this point.

You must realize there is and always will be only 24 hours in a day.

There is also the false belief that if you are busy, you are successful. Because of this myth, many people find themselves putting in more and more time at work and home. It is the "keep up with the Joneses" phenomenon.

In reality, you want to be productive, not just look like it.

Why are you so busy? Why do you find yourself running from one event to another in your life? Often times, busyness is a choice. You might not realize you make that choice every day, but you do. You are busy because you can be. You are busy because you are afraid of your competition. You are busy because you get a natural high from the adrenalin and excitement. You are busy because you let too many leeches into your life...yes the folks that suck the life out of you. You are busy because you let technology run your life. You are busy because it is a status symbol. Lastly, maybe you are busy because you are afraid of being left out.

So, how do you combat all these demands in your life?

One key simple response is to say "no" more often to those things you have control over. If you are committing to too much in your personal life, it will affect your job. You need "down" time at home to rejuvenate and be at your best each and every day.

Stop and think before you say "yes" to something. Think it all the way through. This may be difficult for you, especially if you love to help others, or have a "save the world" mentality. I have learned over the years to ask three key points before making a decision to take on something new:

1) **What are the expectations of my work?**
2) **When do you meet?**
3) **How long is the commitment?**

Then, I completely digest the answers to these questions before making a decision. I also do not immediately make a decision. When asked to commit to something, I respond that I will need some more information about the expectations and time to think it over. I always take at least three days before getting back with a response.

If you don't take the time to think the entire commitment through, you will be making a decision based on emotion. Of course emotion tells you to help! Yet, if you thought it through logically, it may not be in your best interest or the best interest of the asking party or organization.

Recognize 80% of your decisions are based on emotion, while only 20% are based on logic. Take the time to step away and get into the logical decision-making mindset.

By all means, set structure and systems in place. This will allow you to control the demands of your job rather than it controlling you.

QUICK TIP: *Let the answering machine field calls during the evening rush hour at home. Screen your calls at work so you can concentrate on your top priority.*

Angela Esnouf, Creating Order from Chaos
Blackburn South, Victoria, Australia

Chapter 33

ANOTHER BUSINESS MEETING
•••

If the statement, "Let's have a meeting," sounds like the equivalent of fingernails on a chalkboard, please read on. Scott Snair, author of "Stop The Meeting, I Want To Get Off!" states that today's workers spend between 25% and 75% of their workday in meetings. Approximately half of these meetings are unproductive.

There are simple guidelines to help you decide if it is necessary to schedule a meeting. Once necessity has been determined, there are guidelines that ensure the meeting will be interesting and productive.

Schedule a meeting if your team needs interactive communication to resolve issues or share information. If a meeting will help create synergy for the team, schedule it. If a memo or an email will accomplish what your team needs, or if the meeting is simply being used as a morale booster, cancel it. Send the memo or have a party instead. Your employees will call you a hero.

If a meeting is necessary, you and your team need to make it worthwhile. Better meetings result in higher morale, as well as in faster and better decisions. Good meetings start with positive attitudes and team support. Every successful meeting should have the following:

1) **A clearly-stated purpose.** For example: "The purpose of this meeting is to finalize or approve the annual marketing budget." Use words like "finalize" or "approve" instead of "review" or "discuss."

2) Make attendance mandatory. All critical players must be there and be on time.

3) Set guidelines--no cell phones, no blackberries, and no laptops.

4) Set a timetable that states the start time, end time and any break times - and stick to it. Respect your coworkers' time.

5) In advance distribute an agenda that assigns everybody an active role in the meeting and

forces him or her to prepare something in advance. If people feel accountable, they will be more active and attentive during the meeting. Keep this agenda manageable; don't try to tackle too much in too short a timeframe.

6) Assign a Facilitator to maintain order; they will keep the meeting on time and on subject.

7) Designate a Project Manager who will email the meeting summary to all attendees. This will outline all resolved items, and restate who was assigned the responsibility to complete tasks and their deadlines.

8) Only have people attend the meeting who are needed. Don't keep 30 people for 2 hours, when 10 are needed for only the last hour.

9) Every meeting should have conflict. Make your team feel comfortable about stating their opinions-- good or bad--because without conflict people lose interest. If everybody feels that they were respectfully listened to, they will find it easier to support the group's final decision.

Patrick Lencioni, author of "Death By Meeting," suggests that companies divide meetings into four categories:

1) **Daily Check In**: Take five minutes at the beginning of each day. Team members report on what they are doing that day. This saves email and phone time for the remainder of the day. It also allows your team to relay information to co-workers who are out of the office or who call in for updates throughout the day.
2) **Weekly Tactical**: Lasts one hour and is used to resolve or clarify weekly issues.
3) **Monthly Strategic**: Generally two hours long and tackles one topic in depth.
4) **Quarterly Off Site**: For executives to step away from daily, weekly, and monthly issues and focus on long-term objectives.

The solution to meetings is NOT to stop having them, but to make the ones that are necessary better. An interesting, interactive, and properly run meeting is a huge time saver, not a time waster!

QUICK TIP: *Start meetings at unconventional times. Consider starting meetings at oddball times, such as 10:10 am. You will have a better chance of getting everyone there on time rather than running in from a late meeting. If you do this, make sure to adjust your length of meeting time to 50 minutes rather 60 minutes and so on.*

Stephanie LH Calahan, Calahan Solutions, Inc
Bloomington, Illinois

Chapter 34

THE COST OF PAPER

"Paper clutter can quickly accelerate to avalanche stage if there is no system to deal with it."

- eHow.com

The buzzword of the 1990's was "paperless." Computers and electronic storage were to be the new wave of the future. However, because cutting-edge technology has made information easier to obtain, we are generating more paper than ever.

With one push of the "print" key, you can print three or 3000 pages. The information highway has become an addictive resource for many. You literally have all the information in the world available at your fingertips. Unfortunately, many feel the need to print out the information discovered on-line or received in electronic mail. According to

Document Magazine, email is increasing print volumes by 40 percent.

Obviously there is a hard cost associated with printing more documents. The apparent costs are the cost of the paper, the cost of purchasing printers, and the maintenance of printers. Some of the less recognizable hard costs are in the number of copies made and the cost in maintaining those copies. According to PriceWaterhouseCoopers, the average organization makes 19 copies of each document, spends $20 in labor to file each document, and $120 in labor searching for each misfiled document. In some companies, this can be the deciding factor between profit and loss. There is no question it greatly increases expenses for all companies.

For most businesses and households there is a need to retain printed copies of documents. However, to avoid unnecessary expenses, these documents must be maintained in an organized fashion so they can be readily retrieved when needed. With the sheer volume of paper in our society, a clear, efficient, and effective system for processing and maintaining paper must be in place. Systems literally save time, energy, and money.

Managing these costs simply comes down to the decisions made each day: to print or not to print. The urge to print and have this information in your own hot little hands rivals your urge to procrastinate.

The primary question to ask when deciding whether to print is: "Do I really need this information in print form or can I save it on my computer?" If saving on the computer is a viable option, make sure you know how to do this. For the majority of the workforce this training has never been provided. Take the time to educate yourself.

In order to control and reduce costs, education of how to set up systems and process paperwork is a must. Completing an annual productivity system review, and investing in one-on-one organizing and system management, will help corral the ever-increasing cost of paper.

QUICK TIP: Eighty percent of the paper you save *just in case* is never needed again. And if it is, chances are you can recreate or get it from another source. Remember, your trashcan and your shredder are your friends.

High Tech Backup
Kb.htbackup.com

Chapter 35

MAKING THE MOST OF LIMITED WORKSPACE

●●●

How you set up your workspace, at work or in a home office, will determine how effective you are in getting your work done. The physical layout of your office can slow down, or speed up, your efficiency.

Today's workspace requires room for a variety of standard items such as computer, printer, telephone, docking station, stapler, tape dispenser, and so on. Where you locate these items is the key to how productive you may be on a daily basis.

Think of your workspace as real estate. Those areas within arms reach are prime real estate. This will likely include your computer, printer, telephone, and stapler. Only items you access on a daily basis should be located on prime real estate.

Those areas that require you to stretch a little should contain items that are accessed a couple times a week, or several times a month. Some of these items might include tape dispenser, calculator, and reference material.

The areas that require you to get up out of your chair should house items you access a few times a month; and the areas that require a step-stool or a trip down the hallway, should contain items you access occasionally or rarely.

These guidelines hold true for papers and files. For organization sake, all papers or documents should be stored in some type of container such as a file folder, desk tray, basket, bin, or file organizer. Having piles of papers strewn all over your desk not only takes up valuable workspace, but it also clutters your desk and your brain. There is no doubt clutter slows down productivity. In fact, according to the National Association of Professional Organizers, the average executive wastes 6-12 weeks each year looking for misplaced documents. Clutter is the largest culprit for lost documents.

Daily accessed files should be housed on top of your desk, in a file organizer or file drawer that is easily opened and organized so that a document can simply be dropped into the appropriate file. The key here is convenience. If something takes too many steps to perform, you will not do it. Make it simple to file: drop it in a file, or open a drawer, and drop it in.

With the increasing amount of information available on the internet, now is also the time to evaluate the use of the telephone book, calculator, and calendar. Do you use these items electronically on-line now? If so, they no longer need to be within arms reach.

By simply rearranging your workspace, you can save yourself valuable time. Go ahead and test your space. Sit down and stretch out your arm. Are all the items you reach things you use on a daily basis? If not, move them up, or out. Now stand up and reach out your arms. Are the things you reach items you need just a couple times a week, or several times a month? If not, then move them up or out. Continue with the process until the items in your workspace occupy the correct space.

By making the most of your workspace, you can find more time in your day, and maybe even find that document you misplaced last week!

QUICK TIP: Don't have room for an official 'home office'? Put your desk into a closet in the guest room. Add some shelving and other containers to organize supplies and papers. When company comes and the room has to double as the spare bedroom, just close the closet door and it's all hidden away!

Tara Hahn, New Leaf Organizing
Houston, Texas

Chapter 36

PLEASE STOP THE INTERRUPTIONS

"If you allow or encourage constant workflow interruptions, or consistently allow others to place their priorities ahead of your priorities, don't be surprised when you lose control of your day."

-Lynn Wilks, <u>Exploring Productivity</u>

Thanks to Alexander Graham Bell the telephone has become a standard business tool over the past century. When used appropriately, and efficiently, it can be a valuable tool in the workplace.

Planning is a key component for utilizing the telephone in the work environment. According to the National Association of Professional Organizers, a planned telephone call takes seven minutes while an unplanned call takes twelve minutes. Before making a call, be sure to have all potential reference materials in front of you and know specifically what it is you are going to say. If the call involves a great deal of information, create an outline of all the topics that need to be discussed and specific information that needs to be retrieved. If your thoughts are organized, you can make efficient use of your talk time. Likewise, if the party is not available, you will be able to leave a well-organized message on their voicemail.

Utilizing voicemail is a time-saver for both parties involved. If information simply needs to be transferred between two individuals and a discussion does not need to take place, voicemail is highly encouraged. You may even wish to consider making, or returning, these telephone calls when you know you will reach the other parties' voicemail. Transferring information between voicemails takes up much less time than a conversation. Be sure to leave a well-detailed message with the information you need. Make it clear that the other party may simply respond by leaving a detailed message with the information requested. Telephone tag is a waste of time and should be avoided as much as possible.

Use caller ID or have your calls screened. If you know who is calling and you know they are simply calling to give you information you requested, let the phone call go to voicemail. Now you have the information you need, can retrieve it at your pace, and won't waste valuable time conversing on the telephone. A similar technique can be used for call screening too. This method not only reduces talk time, but also reduces lost productivity due to task switching and interruptions.

If you are on the receiving end of a chit-chatty caller, bring the caller to the point by saying, "Thanks for calling; what can I do for you?" This type of question requires an immediate response, and directs the caller to the point. You can also set a time limit on your calls by saying, "I only have five minutes to talk." This opens a door to end the conversation when time *is up.*

Most business calls can be made in five minutes or less. If you are easily distracted, or find yourself spending too much time on the telephone, use an egg timer and set it for five minutes when making, or taking, a call. When the timer goes off, it's time to wrap up the conversation.

If you find yourself caught up in an automated telephone system, you can try pushing zero. Many times, pushing zero will bring you directly to a "live operator" and you can escape from the automated maze.

Taking the time to plan your calls, keeping the conversation focused, utilizing voicemail, and caller ID can lead to being more productive at work. If you engage in a dozen calls a day, shaving five minute off each call results in a savings of one hour each day.

QUICK TIP: Instead of calling the same person multiple times throughout the day, keep a notepad at your desk and jot down items to discuss and make only one call a day.

Pat Roland, Personal Assistant To You,
Cedar Rapids, Iowa

Chapter 37

FIVE STRATEGIES TO IMPROVE PRODUCTIVITY

●●●

"Adopt a new attitude by deliberately choosing how you will spend your time."

-Sara Pedersen, owner of Time To Organize

It is no surprise for you to battle productivity each and every day. With more and more things coming at you, being as productive as possible is a daily challenge. With some basic strategies you will be able to get a better handle on improving your productivity.

Here are five strategies to help improve your productivity:

1) **Eliminate distractions.** Various items on your computer can cause enormous bouts of distraction. In particular, the automatic chime

that you hear when a new email comes into your inbox or a popup on your screen with the same message is an ominous distraction. Turn them off. Recognize that instant messaging and texting are classic distractions. When focusing on a project, turn off the computer, silence the phone, and put on a pair of headphones or earplugs.

2) **Create a timed agenda for daily to-dos.** When you list the 6-10 tasks you are to accomplish on your Daily To-Do List (as discussed in Chapter 31), designate the amount of time you should spend on each task.

3) **Evaluate things that slow you down and then simplify them.** I have a client who found she spent way too much time trying to locate proposals on her desk. She simplified her system, by printing out all her proposals on hot pink paper. Now she can quickly find her proposals, even if they become buried on her desk.

4) **Remove the audio and visual clutter.**

5) **Rotate projects.** You will be more productive if you finish a project before you start another one. If you must have multiple projects going at the same time, close up one project before

starting a new one. In other words, don't dive into multiple projects at the same time.

> **QUICK TIP:** *Use a timer to keep you on task. When the bell goes off, it tells you that you need to stop and focus on something else.*
>
> **Evelyn Gray, Organizing For Success**
> **Alhambra, California**

Chapter 38

DE-STRESS FOR THE HEALTH OF IT

"If you are feeling overworked, exhausted, and depleted, the first step is to let go at work and take care of yourself."

-Julie Morgenstern,
<u>Never Check E-Mail in the Morning</u>

Stress in the workplace can be an endless cycle. Stress at work causes decreased productivity and decreased productivity causes more stress. The cycle continues from there.

If you find yourself stuck in the stress-cycle, continue reading for tips on how to jump off the cycle and get back on the productivity train.

Three of the most important components for managing stress are eating, sleeping, and exercising. It is no secret that the better you manage your stress, the more productive you will be.

Eating nourishes your body and can counteract fatigue and irritability. The key is to eat the right foods at the right times. It is best to eat five or six small daily meals, rather than only two or three larger ones.

There was a reason you had snack time in grade school. Your body needed replenishing so you could concentrate and learn new things. It is the same in the workplace. You still need replenishing, so create a snack time or two at work. During snack time, eat high protein or brain food snacks such as yogurt, cheese, granola and nuts. If you are a bit tense, consider a handful of almonds as they contain natural muscle-relaxing magnesium. Bananas are also a healthy snack choice and they also contain magnesium to help relax tight muscles.

Arriving to work after a refreshing night's sleep will boost productivity and provide motivation for tackling the demands of your job. Seven to eight hours of sleep every night is recommended in order to give your body the rest it needs to rejuvenate. If you find falling asleep difficult consider drinking some warm milk or chamomile tea, as they both create a mild sedating effect. You can top off either of these beverages with some honey, as honey turns off the "alertness" neurotransmitter in your brain. However, use only a small amount of honey, as too much sugar is stimulating. This is just another reason why high sugar snacks during the day may not be a good choice if you are already over-stressed.

Napping also does wonders for productivity and efficiency. A 24-minute powernap is known to increase levels of dopamine in your brain. Dopamine is the brain chemical important for tasks such as focusing, concentration, attention, memory, time-management, decision-making, and prioritizing. If a fuzzy sleep-deprived brain is hindering your productivity, consider a powernap over your lunch hour, or sneak out to your car for a short nap break.

In addition to the cardio-vascular benefits of exercise, the benefit as a stress reliever and brain booster are significant, too. Exercise triggers three key neurotransmitters in your brain: dopamine, norepinephrine, and serotonin. As you know, dopamine is important because it opens up and stimulates the prioritizing and concentrating part of your brain. Norepinephrine and serotonin are known to calm your mood and anxiety levels. To quote John Ratey, M.D., "Exercise is like taking a little bit of Ritalin and Prozac." In other words, exercise creates the natural effect of helping maintain focus and calm your mood. I guess you can think of exercise as a free drug!

So the next time you find your productivity sluggish, consider eating a brain buster snack, taking a powernap, or taking a brisk walk. All of these will help to reduce your stress level and get you back on the productivity train.

QUICK TIP: *Move any time you can...exercise does NOT have to be done in 30 minute segments. Break your exercise routine up into 3- 10 minute segments if that works best for you. If it's hard to exercise away from home, maybe it's time to invest in a piece of exercise equipment for the home. Listen to your self talk. Change negative self talk into positive self talk. Instead of repeating over and over that you hate to exercise, start telling yourself how good you feel after you exercise.*

Mary Beth Helgens, Sisters Health Club
Cedar Rapids, Iowa

Chapter 39

HOW TO HAVE A CLEAN DESK IN ONE WEEK

●●●

If you cringe every time you look at your desk or you spend WAY too much time digging through piles of stuff, it's time to clear off your desk. Starting your day with a clean desk, and a clear mind, is invigorating!

In order to have a clean desk in one week, you need to commit 45 minutes over your lunch hour each day. Yikes! I know I am talking about your lunch hour, but it is only for one week and it will be well worth the investment.

Here's the step-by-step process:

1) **Monday's lunch hour:** Go through your physical file folders. Toss anything you no longer need. Ask yourself, "Can I get this

information somewhere else?" If so, toss it. Consider scanning in items needed for archival storage. If you choose to scan the items, create a "To Scan" folder and place those items in there. Stay a few minutes late tonight to scan in your items, or set aside time on your calendar to do it next week.

2) **Tuesday's lunch hour:** Evaluate your systems for time, paper, and space management. Are they all working? Are they working efficiently and effectively? If not, consider tweaking them or changing them out completely. Make sure you have a clearly marked inbox and outbox.

3) **Wednesday's lunch hour;** Spend the entire 45 minutes focused only on deleting OLD emails. Do not wander into reviewing, or answering new emails.

4) **Thursday's lunch hour:** Devote your 45 minutes today to reading any outstanding magazines, articles, or newspapers. Toss any that are no longer important or that you realistically won't ever read.

5) **Friday's lunch hour:** Go through each item on your desk, one-by-one, and put those items away. If they don't have a current home, then create one. For the work-in-progress (WIPs)

tasks put them away in their appropriate homes and calendar a time to come back and work on them. This overcomes the out-of-sight out-of-mind fear.

Don't put it off, start next Monday! In just a week, you will have more room to work, and you will feel much better about yourself. Now get going!

QUICK TIP: *Schedule a weekly 7-minute "Express Clean-Up" in your Day-Timer planner. That's long enough to get things tidy, but short enough to not be intimidating.*

Kolorkube.com

Chapter 40

ATTACK YOUR READING PILE
●●●

Information and reading materials are abundant. From industry magazines to daily newspapers to internal communications, undoubtedly you have a pile or two of reading materials stacked somewhere in your office.

No question there is some great information buried in that stack, but I suspect many of those items in your pile are months, if not years old. While the information in the reading pile can provide you with some great knowledge, it also drags you down and reduces your productivity.

You not only need a system for attacking your reading material, but also the discipline to tackle your piles on a regular basis. Here are six steps you can follow for managing your reading materials:

1) **Subscribe to only one copy per office.** Not only will this greatly reduce the amount of paper in the office, it will also keep the materials moving along from person to person. Affix a routing tag to the new copy as it arrives and send it on its way. If you are responsible for reading the copy, and passing it onto the next person, it is less likely it will stall in your office for months - or years. Simply knowing someone else is waiting for the copy to be circulated to them is sometimes just the motivation you need to tackle that trade magazine.

2) **Consider assigning information gathering to one person in the office.** Instead of everyone perusing a multitude of magazines and newspapers, have one key individual screen all the reading materials for relevant articles and information. This screening person pulls the important information and pitches the rest. Only the relevant information is forwarded to rest of the organization.

3) **Be selective.** First of all, only subscribe to information that is critical for your job. Secondly, get realistic about your time availability. If 30 minutes a day is all you can allot to reading, you will only get through 2 maybe 3 articles a day. If you have a stack of reading materials, you have months of solid reading time ahead of you. Get real; you do not have three solid months of time to devote to reading. Plus, I have yet to meet anyone who has time each day to sift through their reading pile.

4) **Set guidelines.** Once you have removed yourself from your reading fantasyland, you will recognize you have to let go of most of your reading materials. If your reading materials are daily newspapers or news articles set yourself a guideline of one week. Anything older than a week gets tossed. Recognize that the reason this information is called "news" is that the information is suppose to be "new". If you are reading it months - or years - later, it is not new anymore! For monthly journals, or magazines, two or three months is plenty of time to give yourself to read. If they are more than three months old, toss them because chances are likely you will not have the time to go back and read them.

5) **Tear it out, or make a copy.** If you come across an article that is crucial to your job, do not leave it as part of the magazine or newspaper. Tear out the article. If the magazine does not belong to you, make a photocopy. The key here is to minimize the amount of papers you retain. There is no need to keep an entire magazine for simply one or two articles. Take what you need and then pitch or pass on the magazine.

6) **Scan the important stuff.** If you have processed your reading materials and are left with only the most important and critical reference material, scan that information into your computer. An article saved electronically takes up little space. Be sure to file the article away in an organized fashion in your

computer. You might consider creating a file called "Reading Material" with subfolders for various categories important to your job. Name the files by the title of the individual articles. Besides less paper, the other benefit is the ease in finding the article when you need it. Running a search query on your computer is probably more successful and time efficient than digging through stacks of papers on your desk.

Lastly, keep in mind that information can be found in more than one place. With the internet, you have access to more information than can be found in your stack of reading materials. You literally have tons of information at your fingertips. Besides that, will you really dig out that reference article from months, or years, ago? Or will you just Google the most current information?

> *QUICK TIP: Is having too much to read and do counterproductive to living the life you want? In six months or a year will reading this article, book, etc. really matter to the direction you want your life to go?*
>
> ***Susan Volpe, Home and Organizing
> Sherman Oaks, California***

Chapter 41

STOP THE SCREEN AND LET ME OFF

"The Technology Demon stays on duty all day and all night. It invites you to get lost in its mazes by working or playing long after it's appropriate or useful."

-Geraldine Markel, Ph.D,
<u>Defeating the 8 Demons of</u>
<u>Distraction</u>

While technology may increase the speed you get information, it also complicates matters.

Without doubt, the various technology gadgets like computers, cell phones, Blackberries, iPods, and iPhones have placed higher demands and more stress in your life. If you are like standard

Americans, you are connected 24/7. There is little downtime for yourself. You are always on-call.

The new era of technology has also created some new time management issues. Our society wastes hours on end in a new pastime called "screensucking." Ned Hallowell, M.D., author of Crazy Busy, recently coined this term. Our lives are so enveloped in various technologies that we find ourselves distracted from what really needs to be done. Much of our time is spent engaged with a screen. In addition to the gadgets already listed above, there are the traditional stand by's of televisions and video games, too.

I am sure you can relate to times you started researching one thing on the internet, only to find yourself in a totally different area two hours later. Or, you went into your email box to look up just one email message before heading out to lunch. Twenty-two emails and 75 minutes later, you're still sitting at your desk and the lunch hour is well over.

Dr. Hallowell describes screensucking so well: "Held by a mysterious force, a person can sit long after the work has been done or the show he wanted to watch is over, absently glommed on to the screen, not especially enjoying what he is doing but not able to disconnect and turn off the machine."

Technology is addicting and when not appropriately managed, wastes your time. Screensucking is one of those addictions. So, how do you manage the screensucking? Firstly, you must recognize that screensucking is done unintentionally. No one really says, "Hey, I think I will waste my time wandering around the internet, so I can feel guilty about not getting my work done." Secondly, because it is unintentional, you must intentionally recognize you are susceptible to this phenomenon every time you turn on a screen.

And lastly, you must implement strategies that will snap you back into reality. The best way for doing so is utilizing a timer or alarm clock. Every time you jump onto a screen, and you think there is even the slightest chance you may get sucked in, set the timer. When it goes off, simply ask yourself, "Am I doing what I am suppose to be doing?" Moreover, if time is up, turn off the device.

When technology devices begin to affect relationships and jobs, or strike feelings of panic when without them, it is an indication of a problem. Technology is dominating your life, and you are caught in a dangerous web. Jump off the web, turn off the device, and enjoy some technology-free time.

QUICK TIP: *Schedule your time more effectively; check your email only at scheduled times, practice the 3 R's Read, Respond & Remove as quickly as possible, use all the tools possible in your e-mail software. i.e. calendars, follow up reminders, contacts and don't print messages which just creates another stack of paper.*

Natasha Packer, As You Wish Organizing
Everett, Washington

Chapter 42

HOARDING VS. CLUTTER

•••

When does clutter become "hoarding?" Or better yet, does too much clutter lead to hoarding?

Compulsive hoarding is a potentially serious mental issue. There are thoughts among the scientific community that it's a "wiring" issue of the brain. Some connect it to obsessive-compulsive disorders and others to impulse control disorders.

Hoarding is defined as the acquisition and failure to dispose of large quantities of items, which are of little use or value (Frost & Gross, 2003). However, to the hoarder, these items are considered valuable and needed. This is because the hoarder has a distorted and abnormal view of an item's value. Many times hoarders will determine an item has value simply because someone else finds it to be valuable.

Take this scenario, two friends are shopping at a yard sale (hoarders love the variety and hunting challenge of yard sales), one buys a weed-eater because he/she really needs one. The other, the hoarder, also buys a weed-eater.

Ironically, the hoarder lives in a condo and doesn't have a yard to care for. The weed-eater has no obvious use to the hoarder. However, because the hoarder's friend finds it valuable, the hoarder determines it must be valuable. In fact, the hoarder will create a need, *i.e., I've thought about moving to a home with a yard, so I could need it; I bet my sister could use a new one; or I've been thinking about becoming a seller on ebay, I think I can re-sell it online.* Essentially, some hoarders determine value based on what others perceive as valuable.

Clutter, on the other hand, can be a sign of hoarding. Yet, in many cases, clutter is simply the result of the inability to keep up with the household. Many clutterers do know what has value and can let go of items, but simply have gotten behind on the household chores for whatever reason.

Although there are an estimated 700,000 to 1.4 million people in the United States* thought to have compulsive hoarding syndrome, clutter does not always lead to compulsive hoarding. Nevertheless, clutterers and hoarders both will likely need to consult with a therapist and/or professional organizer for assistance in putting order back into their life.

*According to the Obsessive Compulsive Foundation.

QUICK TIP: *Make a habit of doing certain every day things. This is how non- hoarders are able to manage a household and/or keep an area clean.*

Understanding Obsessive Compulsive Hoarding Disorder

Chapter 43

WHY HIRE AN ORGANIZER?

"Don't confront your enemy alone. Use an army of support for getting organized and staying organized."

> -Judith Kolberg,
> **Conquering Chronic**
> **Disorganization**

The organizing profession has taken off in recent years, mainly because a conglomeration of just-about-everything is easily available. With a couple internet searches you can find most anything you need, and don't need. Plus, there seems to be a big-box store on every corner!

Moreover, technology is making it easier for retailers to market their products. We have 100+ TV channels that all have commercials. Direct mail is easier and less expensive than ever….everything is automated, no more hand addressing, stuffing and mailing. And the internet is loaded with advertising.

To top this off, most (if not all items) manufactured today are made of less expensive material with the idea that the product will be used for a short period of time and replaced with the next best model, style, or hippest color. Essentially, products are made to be disposable.

This creates a problem for many because you feel it is your moral obligation to hang onto everything until it no longer works and then take it apart and use the spare parts for something else…even if it's for "something you may need one day." Before long you find yourself overwhelmed and your home full of clutter.

Is this the right time to seek out an organizer? Our experience over the past nine years is that clients seek out an organizer for three different reasons (and sometimes a combination of any of the three):

1) **I don't know how to organize my clutter.** Organization is a learned skill. No where in life do you "formally" learn it. (However, there is current progress being made at introducing organization education in a structured format in the elementary and college levels). Like anything else, some of you have more of a natural knack than others. For those that don't have the knack, an organizer is the perfect teacher for helping learn those skills.

2) **I have way too much stuff and it's too much work to do it on my own.** Often even if you "know" how to do it, there is way too much work to physically do it all on your own. Additionally, because there is so much to organize, it is too overwhelming and emotionally draining. In this situation, a skilled professional organizer can help with the organizing, while also coaching and providing support through the challenging issues that will be encountered.

3) **I need the motivation.** Like so many other things you really don't want to do, you put "organizing" on the back burner. However, if you have an appointment scheduled with an organizer, it will get done. It's just the extra kick in the pants you might need.

QUICK TIP: An organizer offers fresh, objective ideas helping you move past overwhelming feelings.
They will assist in creating new systems and plans for dealing with the stuff of life, in business and at home.

An organizer offers non-biased eyes and ears to your situation(s). Together, you can create new systems and plans that will empower you to lead a more stress free and productive life in business and at home.

Anita Van Dyke,
Marion, Iowa

Appendix 1

●●●

References

Wall Street Journal: One hour is wasted everyday simply because of disorganization.

Author unknown: The easiest way to get something done is to begin.

Xplor International: The amount of paper printed in the world more than doubled from 1995 to 2005.

Insurance depreciation information courtesy of Claimspages.com

According to the Bureau of Transportation, 10,089 bags were lost, or delayed, daily in August 2006.

There is a great free template for household budgets available at http://www.vertex42.com/ExcelTemplates/monthly-household-budget.html

Scott Snair, author of "Stop The Meeting, I Want To Get Off!," states that today's workers spend between 25% and 75% of their workday in meetings.

According to Document Magazine, email is increasing print volumes by 40 percent.

According to PriceWaterhouseCoopers, the average organization makes 19 copies of each document, spends $20 in labor to file each document, and $120 in labor searching for each misfiled document.

According to the National Association of Professional Organizers, the average executive wastes 6-12 weeks each year looking for misplaced documents.

According to the National Association of Professional Organizers, a planned telephone call takes seven minutes while an unplanned call takes twelve minutes.

Hoarding is defined as the acquisition and failure to dispose of large quantities of items, which are of little use or value (Frost & Gross, 2003)

Appendix 2

●●●

Resources

Where to find a Professional Organizer:
www. Napo.net

Where to get ADHD help: www.ADD.org

Other resources:

www.freecycle.org

www.Goodwill.com

www.SalvationArmyUSA.org

www.Ebay.com

www.CraigsList.com

www.mfyuc.com

www.tsa.gov

www.getmoredone.com

www.zeromillion.com/business/management/delega
ting-work.html

www.TheOrganizingChoice.com

Appendix 3

●●●

Summary of Organizing Tips

Organizing gives you more time to do what you love.
Chances are good the first thing you want to do at the end of
the day or on the weekend does not involve managing piles
or dealing with clutter. So this is one of the most powerful
motivations for getting (and staying) organized: when you no
longer have to devote time, thought, and energy to corralling
the excess stuff around you, you can devote that time,
thought, and energy to the people, activities, and events that
you love.

Emily Wilska, The Organized Life
San Francisco, California
www.OrganizeLlife.org

Finish all projects completely before moving on to another.
This includes putting away all tools and supplies used and
cleaning the area where the project was worked on. This
helps to eliminate the backsliding effect. Take an extra few
moments now and you won't have to take a day later to catch
up.

Sherri Papich, Organize Your Life LLC,
Springville, New York
www.YouCanOrganizeYourLife.com

People often think "It takes so much time!" Remember the title of this book? Set a timer for 2 minutes a day and tackle one area of your home that's bothering you. In the long run, the time you set aside to get organized will more than pay off!

Sally Ficken
Cedar Rapids, Iowa

Feeling overwhelmed by organizing a large room? Focus on ONE area in that room, such as a bookcase or closet area. Gradually move around that room organizing, as your time permits, until the whole room is completed!

Gaylynn Winn, Organize it…One Room at a Time,
Columbia, Missouri

\
Have your recycle bin, letter opener and mail center together preferably near your door. That way, you can process your mail before it gets further than your hallway.

Zele Avradopoulos, Zorganize,
Waltham, Massachustts
www.Zorganize.net

Keep a notebook with you and remember to also put one next to your bed so you won't forget any great ideas.

Joetta Tucker, My Organizing Friend,
Geneva, New York
www.MyOrganizingFriend.com

For the filing challenged, create a fun, inspiring category. For instance, instead of 401k, stocks, etc. call it Wealth. It's much more empowering.

Karen Flagg, Organize This! LLC,
Austin, Texas
www.OrganizeThisAustin.com

Organizing is more about making decisions than it is about removing clutter. Determine how each item of yours makes you feel, and then you can make informed decisions about whether you really need it in your space or life. Once you start making these decisions you will gain more confidence and feel great.

Maggie Knack, A Knack for Organizing,
Edina, Minnesota

Put things where you use them. For example, if your laundry room is on the same floor as your bedroom put a hook near the dryer and laundry bin. I get ready for morning by putting my outfit on the hook. In the winter, a few minutes before bedtime, I put my nightgown in the dryer so it is toasty warm. I drop my dirty clothes in the laundry basket because it is right there. In the morning, my clothes are already there waiting for me and the hook is now free for my night clothes.

Rie Brosco, RieOrganize!,
Philadelphia, Pennsylvania
www.RieOrganize.com

Fasten a safety pin to the bottom right corner seam of your fitted sheets. This will save time and frustration trying to figure out the top and bottom from the sides each time you change the bed.

Betty Arnold, The Organizing Queen,
Tampa, Florida
www.OrgQueen.com

Use a CD organizer that straps to the visor in your car to hold your retail coupons; i.e. Bed, Bath & Beyond and other retail stores!

Dawna Hall, Organize ME!,
Portland, Maine
www.OrganizeMaine.com

Make your entryway an organization zone. Have a place for keys, mail, and backpacks. Get a bench with cubbies or a hall tree with hooks for a simple way to unload the day in an organized way.

Lisa Tella, Neat Chic Organizing,
Ballwin, Missouri

When you have an old washing machine or dryer to get rid of, call your local waste management company and they might come and pick it for a minimal fee CURBSIDE!!

MaSanda LaRa Gadd, HeartVisions,
Bothell, Washington
www.HeartVisions.com

Don't succumb to large quantity purchasing simply because it's a good deal. Purchase in quantity only when you have space for that item.

Brenda McElroy, Organized By Choice,
Fresno, California
www.OrganizedByChoice.com

Finding a charity that is close to your heart might help you rid of excess easier. Local schools or nursing homes can usually use art supplies and/or books. Food pantries or shelters can use many necessities. Many organizations have yearly garage sales to benefit their cause and will accept just about anything that is clean and unbroken. If you are an animal lover, contact your local pet shelter to see what they will accept.

Sherri Papich, Organize Your Life LLC,
Springville, New York
www.YouCanOrganizeYourLife.com

Keep an extra plastic grocery bag in your vehicle to use for trash. For even more convenience, put a bag holder in your garage.

Joetta Tucker, My Organizing Friend
Geneva, New York
www.MyOrganizingFriend.com

When traveling stuff socks and other small items into shoes to maximize space and offer support to your shoes.

Katherine Lawerence, Space Matters
Richmond, Virginia
www.MySpaceMatters.com

When traveling with young children pack each daily outfit in a store brand gallon size zipper bags you can easily fit a diaper, washcloth, socks, shirt and pants. It will save you time getting dressed at a relatives' home or hotel. You can also pack extra diapers, wipes, etc. in zipper bags. This also saves room in your suitcase because you can squeeze all the air out and create flat "packages" for packing (not to mention saving spills or messy baggage checks). On the way home, the bags can be used for dirty clothes, local purchases or liquids in the diaper bag/carry on. Back home you can use the bags for a final time on dog walks.

Carolyn Anderson Fermann, Simply Organized Life
Dexter, Michigan
www.SimplyOrganizedLife.com

Make extra breakfast food and freeze it for a busy morning. Extra pancakes, muffins, breakfast casserole, etc can really be a lifesaver when you are short on time!

Joetta Tucker, My Organizing Friend
Geneva, New York
www.MyOrganizingFriend.com

Do you have space in your cabinets to hold the holiday dishes? If not - simply rotate them for the season. Store your regular dishes whenever you bring out the holiday dishes.

Holiday recipes along with your holiday dishes can be kept in storage until next year

Joetta Tucker, My Organizing Friend
Geneva, New York
www.MyOrganizingFriend.com

Plan all dinners for the week, with your family if possible. Write your grocery list from the menus, fill in other needed items then go grocery shopping ONCE a week! If it's not on the list, it doesn't get purchased until the next week.

Donna Olsen, From Chaos to Calm
Brockport, New York
www.FromChaosToCalm.org

Think of your home as a business. Your items (clutter) are the employees. Interview each item. If one is not "working" for you, or does not have a place within your home daily, weekly, monthly, or yearly. FIRE IT! ... now get it out of your home.

Deborah Erickson, No Where But Up, Organizing
Hemlock, Michigan
www.NoWhereButUp.com

Maximize your kitchen storage space by having multifunctional utensils. Donate single purpose items that take up valuable space and rarely get used.

Stephanie Manawil, Organized in Style
Orange County, California
www.OrganizedInStyle.com

Try de-cluttering your linen closet. Check with local animal shelters to see if they have a need for your old towels, blankets and sheets. A local shelter can be found at www.pets911.com. They may also appreciate cleaning products that you've kept, but don't use.

Joetta Tucker, My Organizing Friend
Geneva, New York
www.MyOrganizingFriend.com

Where is your critical information? If a disaster occurred could you pick it up and leave without having to hunt for it? If not, how can you correct that?

Teresa Spruill
Spruill Money Management and Organization Services
Smithsburg, Maryland

To help remember birthdays and other important reoccurring events, buy a small hanging calendar (about 7" x 14" when open) & hang on your refrigerator for each month put a 3" x 3" Post-it® note and list the birthdays, anniversaries & repeat for each month. If someone's birthday is the first of the month, put them on the previous month's note. Then you can send a card in time. When the month is over, store the Post-it® note on the last page of the calendar for re-use next year.

Cathy Bock, Chaos Tamers LLC
Northbrook, Illinois
www.ChaosTamers.com

Are you hanging onto manuals for every item you've EVER owned? Well - recycle them and free up space! If you need one, you can download just about any owner's manual for free at www.safemanuals.com.

Joetta Tucker, My Organizing Friend
Geneva, New York
www.MyOrganizingFriend.com

Dedicate just 15 minutes per day to straightening up, and the clutter won't reach overwhelming proportions!

Lauren Silverman, Moreganized
Skokie, Illinois

I know my personality type very well, and I require a little pressure to meet my deadlines. So when I'm tempted to procrastinate, I look for ways to turn the task or project into a game and find ways to make it FUN! It may be as simple as putting the paperwork in a bright colored file folder and printing out a fun piece of clipart and taping it to the front. Or it may mean breaking the project into smaller chunks and celebrating the completion of each chunk with a small incentive of some sort. Focusing on the RELIEF of finally getting the project completed, though, is sometimes the BEST incentive of all.

Julie Perrine, CPS/CAP, MBTI Certified
Founder and CEO of All Things Admin
Hiawatha, Iowa
www.AllThingsAdmin.com

Create a master list in excel. A master list is a master list of everything you have to do. You may want to sort personal vs. business or create two separate lists. It could also be sorted by season or categories.

Eileen Roth, Everything in Its Place,
Scottsdale, Arizona
www.EverythingInItsPlace.net

Let the answering machine field calls during the evening rush hour at home. Screen your calls at work so you can concentrate on your top priority.

Angela Esnouf, Creating Order from Chaos
Blackburn South, Victoria, Australia
www.CreatingOrder.com.au

Start meetings at unconventional times. Consider starting meetings at oddball times, such as 10:10 am. You will have a better chance of getting everyone there on time rather than running in from a late meeting. If you do this, make sure to adjust your length of meeting time to 50 minutes rather 60 minutes and so on.

Stephanie LH Calahan, Calahan Solutions, Inc
Bloomington, Illinois
www.calahansolutions.com

Eighty percent of the paper you save "just in case" is never needed again. And if it is, chances are you can recreate or get it from another source. Remember, your trashcan and your shredder are your friends.

High Tech Backup
Kb.htbackup.com

Don't have room for an official 'home office'? Put your desk into a closet in the guest room. Add some shelving and other containers to organize supplies and papers. When company comes and the room has to double as the spare bedroom, just close the closet door and it's all hidden away!

Tara Hahn, New Leaf Organizing
Houston, Texas
www.NewLeafOrg.com

Instead of calling the same person multiple times throughout the day, keep a notepad at your desk and jot down items to discuss and make only one call a day.

Pat Roland, Personal Assistant To You,
Cedar Rapids, Iowa
www.PersonalAssistantToYou.com

Use a timer to keep you on task. When the bell goes off, it tells you that you need to stop and focus on something else.

Evelyn Gray, Organizing For Success
Alhambra, California
www.EvelynGray.com

Move any time you can...exercise does NOT have to be done in 30 minute segments. Break your exercise routine up into 3- 10 minute segments if that works best for you. If it's hard to exercise away from home, maybe it's time to invest in a piece of exercise equipment for the home. Listen to your self talk. Change negative self talk into positive self talk. Instead of repeating over and over that you hate to exercise, start telling yourself how good you feel after you exercise.

Mary Beth Helgens, Sisters Health Club
Cedar Rapids, Iowa
www.SistersHealthClub.com

Schedule a weekly 7-minute "Express Clean-Up" in your Day-Timer planner. That's long enough to get things tidy, but short enough to not be intimidating.

Kolorkube.com

Is having too much to read and do counterproductive to living the life you want? In six months or a year will reading this article, book, etc. really matter to the direction you want your life to go?

Susan Volpe, Home and Organizing
Sherman Oaks, California

Schedule your time more effectively; check your email only at scheduled times, practice the 3 R's Read, Respond &

Remove as quickly as possible, use all the tools possible in your e-mail software. i.e. calendars, follow up reminders, contacts and don't print messages which just creates another stack of paper.

Natasha Packer, As You Wish Organizing
Everett, Washington
www.OrganizingAsYouWish.com

Make a habit of doing certain every day things. This is how non- hoarders are able to manage a household and/or keep an area clean.

Understanding Obsessive
Compulsive Hoarding Disorder
http://understanding_ocd.tripod.com

An organizer offers fresh, objective ideas helping you move past overwhelming feelings. They will assist in creating new systems and plans for dealing with the stuff of life, in business and at home.
An organizer offers non-biased eyes and ears to your situation(s). Together, you can create new systems and plans that will empower you to lead a more stress free and productive life in business and at home.

Anita Van Dyke, Get Organized! LLC
Marion, Iowa
www.TheOrganizingChoice.com

Products

Home Operations Made Easy
This *data CD* is your family command center. More than 75 checklists and forms to help you find more time for your life.

Productivity Power Points: Dealing with the Clutter
Audio CD presented by Becky Esker highlights Clutter and what to do with it. A must for those wanting to simplify and get rid of the clutter!

Set the Stage: Home Staging Tips
Set the Stage *Audio CD* presented by Becky Esker outlines simple steps needed to increase the value of your home and get your top dollar!

Organizing Tips & Strategies for ADHD
If you have ADHD, traditional organizing strategies do not work for you! Learn non-traditional tips and strategies for managing organization at work and in the office. *Audio CD* is specifically geared towards those with ADHD.

Year Round Spring Organizing
Basic organizing tips and strategies for getting your home organized and most importantly keeping it organized! On this *DVD* organizing expert Becky Esker gives you hands on information you can put in action right away!

Financial Organizing & Budgeting for the Home
Not sure what financial documents you need to keep, so you keep them all? Then this *audio CD* is for you! Discover what financial papers you can toss and which ones you really need.

All products available at www.TheOrganizingChoice.com

About the Author

●●●

Becky Esker is the owner and founder of Get Organized! L.L.C., a professional organizing service located in Cedar Rapids, Iowa. Get Organized! provides services to those in the greater Eastern Iowa area and also serves those all over the world through its website.

In addition to earning the Certified Professional Organizing (CPO®) designation, Becky also holds her Certificate of Study in Chronic Disorganization and has completed the necessary coursework for her Certificate of Study in Basic ADD Issues with the CD client. She made her first national speaking appearance in July 2008 at the 13th National Attention Deficit Disorder Association Conference in Minneapolis and subsequent national speaking appearances at the National Association of Professional Organizers Midwest Conference in Chicago, the Future Business Leaders of America conference in Minneapolis and the Chicago Home School Expo.

Becky frequently appears on news stations and radio shows. She has been the featured guest on several different live morning shows, has been a regular contributor to *The Edge Business Magazine* and *City Revealed,* and was recently featured as the selected professional organizer in an episode of Hoarding: Buried Alive that originally aired on the TLC network in March 2011.

22993194R00112

Made in the USA
Charleston, SC
09 October 2013